CLIMBING
BRANDON

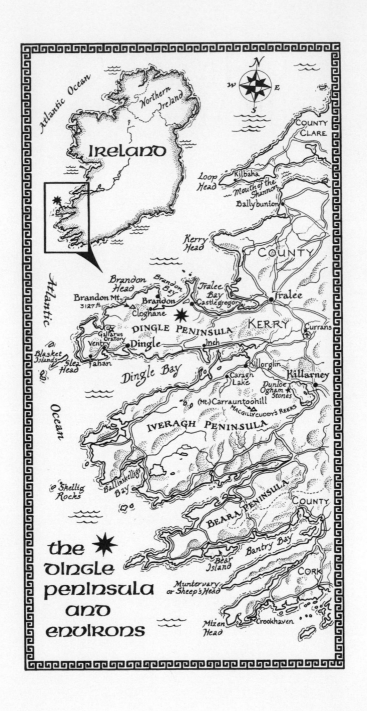

the ✳ DINGLE PENINSULA AND ENVIRONS

CLIMBING BRANDON

Science and Faith on Ireland's Holy Mountain

CHET RAYMO

WALKER & COMPANY
NEW YORK

First published in the United States of America in 2004 by Walker Publishing Company, Inc.

Published simultaneously in Canada by Fitzhenry and Whiteside, Markham, Ontario L3R 4T8

For information about permission to reproduce selections from this book, write to Permissions, Walker & Company, 104 Fifth Avenue, New York, New York 10011.

Library of Congress Cataloging-in-Publication Data
available upon request
ISBN 0-8027-1433-1

Book design by Maura Fadden Rosenthal/Mspace*ny*
Illustrations by Laura Hartman Maestro

Visit Walker & Company's Web site at www.walkerbooks.com

Printed in the United States of America
2   4   6   8   10   9   7   5   3   1

CONTENTS

PREFACE ix

1   BRANDON: BETWEEN HEAVEN & EARTH   1

2   CLOGHANE: TWILIGHT OF THE GODS   21

3   FAHA: LAND OF MILK & HONEY   43

4   BINN NA PORT: THE WILD & THE HOLY   63

5   COUMAKNOCK: MOUNTAIN GLOOM,
    MOUNTAIN GLORY   83

6   SUMMIT: DISCOVERY OF IGNORANCE   105

7   ATLANTIC: THE NEW STORY   125

8   GALLARUS: A NEST BESIDE THY ALTAR   147

ACKNOWLEDGMENTS   169
NOTES   171
INDEX   177

PREFACE

I FIRST CLIMBED MOUNT BRANDON thirty-two years
ago when I came with my family to the west coast of Ireland for a sabbatical year from teaching at Stonehill College in Massachusetts. We rented a charming house on
the edge of the sea, not far from the mountain's base,
enrolled the children in school in Dingle, and I settled
down to study and write. The mountain, meanwhile, was
simply *there*. No matter where you are on the Dingle
Peninsula, Brandon dominates your visual field—a great,
black, boggy, cloud-capped hump rising from the sea and
nearly cutting the peninsula in half. Days passed. Weeks.
The mountain called. The call was impossible to resist.

I climbed Brandon the first time alone, up the old pilgrim path from Ballybrack at the mountain's western
foot. The summit was in cloud, as usual. There were no
views, other than a terrifying glimpse down into the
misty corrie that precipitously interrupts the summit on
the east. So I sat there, in the cloud, munching a candy
bar, and thinking, "Well, done that." But of course I was
not done with the mountain. Or rather, the mountain
was not done with me. It would call me back again and
again. During the year of my Irish sabbatical, I climbed
the mountain half a dozen times.

Since that first visit to the Dingle Peninsula, I have
returned every year and, since 1980, have owned a home

near Dingle town where I spend the summers. I have climbed the mountain perhaps a hundred times, by every practical path. Twenty years ago, it was mostly farmers I met on the mountain, with their dogs, chasing sheep. Today the mountain attracts recreational hill walkers from all over the world; it is a wonderful place to encounter the natural history of Ireland, the flora and fauna, the myths and legends, the sometimes joyous and sometimes grief-scarred history of the people. Every footstep recalls the passage of Celtic warriors and Christian saints, soldiers of the English Crown and the native Irish they drove into the hills, nineteenth-century rack-rent landlords and twentieth-century revolutionaries.

My own interest in the mountain is twofold: It is a landscape of great scientific interest, revealing in its crumpled strata and glacially scarred features much of the geologic history of Ireland; it is also a landscape of great religious significance, one of Ireland's holy mountains, and a microcosm of Ireland's Celtic soul. This is a place where nineteenth-century geologists debated the meaning of the twisted strata and helped unravel the surprising history of the ice ages; and this is a place where early medieval saints repaired to encounter their God. Two geographies—one physical, one spiritual—are interwoven on the mountain in ways, it seems to me, that have a particular relevance for our times. I have taken the mountain as the nexus of several threads in Western thought—Celtic polytheism, Christian monotheism, and scientific empiricism—for which it serves nicely. In particular, I have sought on the mountain ways of easing the tension that resounds in Western culture between empirical knowledge and traditional faith.

Nearly two thousand years ago men and women who lived on the Celtic fringe of Europe grappled with this same tension and—for several extraordinary centuries—lived in a way that seamlessly celebrated both reason and mystery. Ireland was converted to Christianity, traditionally by Patrick, in the fifth century A.D. The Norsemen arrived in the ninth century and established colonies around the coast. The period between is sometimes called the Age of Saints and Scholars, and Ireland was then home to a culture—and a kind of Christianity—that was unique in Europe. It was a culture and a faith intensely intellectual yet fiercely attuned to ineffable intimations of nature, skeptical yet celebratory, grounded in the here and now and open to infinity. On Mount Brandon I found happy traces of that time, and ways to accommodate apparently contending demands of head and heart.

CLIMBING
BRANDON

BRANDON
BETWEEN HEAVEN & EARTH

apple tree branch

Thousands of years ago, in a time recorded only by legend, Bran, son of the Irish king Febal, was walking near his father's royal palace when he was lulled to sleep by mysterious music. When he woke, he found beside him a silver branch with white blossoms. He took the branch into the palace, and there a woman appeared to him and his company, inviting him to visit a world of wonder and delight that lay beyond the Western Sea—the Land of the Women—where treachery, sorrow, sickness, and death are unknown. As she prepared to take her leave, the branch of blossoms magically leaped from Bran's hand to hers, and—*poof*—she was gone. What red-blooded Irishman could resist such an invitation, delivered by a beautiful maiden in exotic dress? Bran wasted no time preparing a boat. The very next day he set out to sea with a crew of three times nine men and eventually arrived with his cohort at the promised isle. They found an elegant house prepared for their arrival, with thrice nine maidens and thrice nine beds, and of course the lady who had invited Bran was there. The voyagers stayed for what seemed to them only a year, but in fact centuries passed. At last, homesick—and perhaps a bit weary of paradise—Bran and his crew set out for home, but not before the woman who issued the invitation warned him not to set foot on Irish soil.

According to local tradition, the returning voyagers made landfall at a place now called Brandon Point, at the foot of Mount Brandon, in southwest Ireland. One of the party, Nechtan by name, impetuously leaped ashore—and collapsed into a heap of dust! No other mariner dared risk a landing. From his place in the boat, Bran shouted out the story of his adventures to people who had gathered on the shore. Then he sailed off into the sunset, with his companions, never to be heard from again.

Was the branch of white blossoms that the fairy lady used to entice Bran westward a staff of apple flowers, as asserted by the standard version of the story? In Irish lore, the apple tree was revered as a symbol of the delights of the otherworld—of fertility, replenishment, and healing. Legend tells of an island in the sea west of Ireland known as Eamhain Abhlach (Land of Apples), and apples (sometimes golden) play roles in other tales of mysterious seduction. British myth, too, has the story of Avalon, the Island of Apples, to which King Arthur was brought to recover from his wounds. Certainly, the apple tree was recognized in ancient Irish law as one of the seven "nobles of the wood," valued for its delicious fruit, with severe penalties attached to its cutting or uprooting.

Or perhaps the branch of white blossoms was hawthorn, the tree that makes the Irish countryside blaze white each spring, every hedgerow a gushing stream of snowy blossoms. A "commoner of the wood," to be sure, but long associated with fairy folk and magical powers. The hawthorn tree was considered unlucky, and if hawthorn was the blossom of the original tale, it may have foretold Bran's ultimate fate, rather than his pleasant sojourn with his companions in the arms of fairy lovers.

Today, Brandon Point, where the returning voyagers approached the shore, is at the end of a narrow road that passes through the villages of Cloghane and Brandon on Ireland's Dingle Peninsula; it is as remote a spot as you are likely to find in County Kerry or throughout the island. Spectacular cliffs, pink with thrift and raucous with the calls of diving birds, fall into the sea. Waves roll endlessly from the western horizon, and one can easily imagine Bran bobbing there in his boat, shouting out the story of the thrice nine maidens and thrice nine beds to his spellbound audience. Turn around, face away from the sea, and a wall of mountain rises before you, mist-shrouded and forbidding, part of the ring of mountains that is Ireland's seaward battlements.

THE TOPOGRAPHY OF IRELAND RESEMBLES a bowl, with a low, fertile limestone interior and a mountainous rim of resistant sandstone and quartz. A few solitary inland prominences have played special roles in Irish history: The Hill of Tara comes to mind, traditional home of ancient Irish kings; and the Rock of Cashel, with its present crown of medieval structures. But it is around the coasts that Ireland shrugs up the boggy shoulders that have long been the strongholds of "the real Ireland," Catholic Ireland, the Ireland of the Gaels.

When Oliver Cromwell conquered Ireland in the seventeenth century, he parceled out the rich interior grasslands to his Protestant English army, banishing the native Catholic Irish "to hell or Connacht." Connacht is the mountainous western province dominated by such familiar peaks as Croagh Patrick and the Twelve Bens of Connemara. The land among these crags was deemed by the English as of not much use for other than stray sheep or Catholics. So too the mountains farther south in the province of Munster became refuges for a conquered people, and they remain today repositories of Gaelic folklore and language.

The westernmost of Ireland's peaks is cloud-capped Mount Brandon, lifting its summit 3,127 feet into the wet Atlantic air. The Gaelic language is still spoken on its flanks, and its glens have a scraggy wildness that makes hell or Connacht seem civilized by comparison. The mountain's black hump rises from rocky fields and gray water near the end of the Dingle Peninsula. It is not the highest mountain in Ireland; that distinction—by a few begrudged feet—belongs to Carrantuohill on the Iveragh Peninsula across Dingle Bay. But Carrantuohill stands among a cluster of high peaks, collectively called the Macgillicuddy Reeks, and its lofty precedence is somewhat disguised by company. Brandon lords it alone over a narrow thumb of land jutting into the sea, and its solitary prominence more than makes up for its somewhat lesser height. Except for a few recent plantations of evergreens at low altitudes, the sides and summit of the mountain are treeless. Experienced walkers are pretty much free to ramble wherever they please, but neophytes best keep to well-trodden paths lest they go astray in mist.

Some say that Mount Brandon takes its name from Bran, the mythic voyager to the Land of the Women. More likely the name recalls the more firmly historical Saint Brendan, known as the Navigator, who was born not far away near the present city of Tralee in the year

484 (or thereabouts), and who late in his life took sail in an oxskin boat from a cove at the base of the mountain on a seven-year voyage in search of the Isles of the Blest. It is claimed that Brendan and his companions "discovered America," but there is no reliable evidence that the voyage took place at all. Nevertheless, Brendan's tale is a compelling metaphor for the journey that carries us all from birth to death, and, for some, in hope, to eternity beyond.

Brendan was one of many highly educated monks of the early Middle Ages who made their home on the rugged west coast of Ireland, facing out into the rain-lashed, fog-shrouded Western Sea. Somewhere beyond those gray mists lay the Isles of the Blest, those holy men believed, a place of rest and happiness. Was it a *literal* paradise they sought in the apparently boundless waters of the west? Certainly, in those oceanic vistas they sensed the majesty of their God, immanent in wind and wave. In solitude and prayer they sought to know Him. To that end they built huts and oratories of unmortared stone in the westernmost reaches of Europe and focused their attention on the far horizon. Brendan is supposed to have built an oratory, a place of prayer, at Shanakeel (Old Church), at the foot of Mount Brandon, and on the summit of the mountain to this day there are remnants of a stone structure said to be associated with the saint.

Medieval tales of the Isles of the Blest, or Land of Delight, may have had a factual source, perhaps in stories derived from Phoenician sailors blown far out into the Atlantic during voyages beyond the Pillars of Hercules (the Straits of Gibraltar), and who found themselves among the Azores or Cape Verde Islands. In the minds of the Irish monks, rumors of islands in the west might have been conflated with even more ancient Celtic myths of a paradise where the Sun goes in its setting. So rich is early Irish mythology with tales of westward voyaging that it sometimes seems there might have been no one left behind to mind hearth and home. Whatever the reason for the monks' pious westerning, hope and fear conspired to give their faith in eternal salvation a geographic referent. Whereas continental Christians looked for heaven in the sky above, the Irish cast their longing gaze at the sea horizon. Every wave that crashed upon the rockbound pediment of Mount Brandon roared a salvic promise that Brendan and his contemporaries were predisposed by learning and tradition to hear.

The corollary of this shift of faith from the vertical to the horizontal was a concept of God that emphasized immanence over transcendence. An uneasy tension between God's immanence and transcendence resonates through the history of Christianity. Catholicism places a strong (although not predominant) emphasis on immanence, as evidenced by the church's sacramental system; its fondness for incense, bells, candles, relics, statues, and stained glass; its reposing of divine authority in popes and councils. Protestantism, by contrast, stresses the relatively disembodied Word and the wholly otherness of God, and can be partly understood as a protest against the Catholic fondness for material embodiments of things divine. In the Protestant view, Catholicism sins by idolatry, finding God everywhere. In the Catholic view, Protestantism drifts toward atheism by finding God nowhere; God becomes so other that he dissolves into nothingness. Of course, these respective views are generalizations, and in both traditions the two aspects of God are mingled.

My early Roman Catholic schooling affirmed God's transcendence, even as it immersed us in a heady atmosphere of candlelight and pungent smoke. My teachers and spiritual guides—mainly nuns and priests of Irish origin or descent—focused our attention on spirit, not matter; the fate of our immortal and immaterial souls was to be our constant concern. They directed our vision upward, away from the Earth, and even if we were told not to take a celestial heaven literally, it was made clear to us that the fallen world of matter was not the domicile of divinity. What a surprise, then, to discover among the Irish Christians of Brendan's era a *horizontal* vision, a gazing into sea fog and rolling waves, a celebration of the here and now, a longing to pass across, not upward but westward.

SEVERAL HUNDRED MILLION YEARS AGO, Brendan would not have required a voyage of seven years to reach America. By keeping to the higher ground, he might have walked there from Ireland dry shod. At that time North America and Europe were part of a single landmass geologists call the Old Red Sandstone Continent. The part of that continent that is now the Dingle Peninsula was then an inland basin, and sands, muds, and pebbles eroded from the surrounding uplands were deposited on the floor of that basin. These eventually became the layered rocks that are the backbone of the Dingle Peninsula: sandstones, mudstones, and conglomerates, gritty, well consolidated, and resistant. Meanwhile, to the south, the drifting continent of Africa was nudging northward, squeezing up against the underbelly of Europe and pushing the floor of an intervening sea back into the interior of the Earth. A great mountain range was lifted skyward, the ancestral Alps. Farther north, behind the jagged peaks, the crust of the Earth was more gently crumpled in wavelike folds, like a carpet pushed from its edge. These folds reveal themselves today in the five rocky fingers of land and intervening bays that are the southwest coast of Ireland. Mount Brandon, like its rival Carrantuohill across Dingle Bay, is the eroded stump of what was once a much higher peak, the floor of a sedimentary basin forced upward.

The folds of these layered rocks are dramatically revealed in the deep glacier-carved valleys that hang on the eastern side of Mount Brandon. Here, an old pilgrim path makes its way to the summit from the village of Faha on the slope of the mountain above Brandon Bay. The path begins at a shrine of the Virgin, where a statue of Saint Brendan looks out from a niche at the Virgin's right hand. Here pilgrims gathered in years gone by on May 16, the saint's feast, to commence in prayer their climb to the top. (Another climb, celebrating a different feast, takes place in summer.) The mountain is still climbed by pilgrims on the Sunday nearest Brendan's feast day, but today most often from the west, on the track from Ballybrack, a gentler and less perilous ascent. In fact, after a decades-long decline in interest, the annual religious pilgrimages up Brandon seem to be attracting more participants—the pious old as always, but also the educated young, who make up in their enthusiasm for an inspiring landscape what they might lack in religious conviction.

Holy mountains figure strongly in the Irish religious imagination. Hardly a summit in Ireland lacks its cross or shrine, and many a path to a summit is marked with Stations of the Cross. Saint Patrick, of course, stands highest in the Irish pantheon of saints, and his mountain in Mayo, Croagh Patrick, is the island's best-known place of pilgrimage. Each year on the last Sunday of July, Reek Sunday (a *reek* is a mountain in Irish popular speech, a variant of *rick,* a heap or pile, as in *peat rick*), thousands of devout trekkers, young and old, climb to the summit where Patrick is said to have made a forty-day solitary vigil in the year A.D. 441. Croagh Patrick was almost certainly "holy" long before Patrick arrived to convert the Irish to Christianity, and the same is true for Mount Brandon. The spirits of Irish warrior heroes of pre-Christian times, including the voyager Bran, share those misty ridges with Brendan's Christian deity. Some places draw us into their thrall because of their inherent aura of majesty and mystery, and this was almost certainly true of Croagh Patrick and Mount Brandon since the earliest arrival of humans in Ireland.

It is a rare day when the summit of Mount Brandon is not capped with cloud, and anyone who lived near the mountain's foot in olden times must have considered its upper slopes a place of formidable mystery. When Brendan went there to build his oratory, he surely went with some trepidation, as if he were entering upon the domain of ancient gods whose influence had not yet been entirely dissipated by the preaching of the Gospel. Saints and holy men and women have long ascended mountains seeking the divine. Moses received the law on Mount Sinai, where God appeared in cloud and fire. Mount Zion at Jerusalem is the site of the temple that would be Yahweh's earthly abode. The life of Jesus, too, especially as described by Matthew, is punctuated with high places: the "high mountain" where he was taken by Satan during his desert fast, the place of his sermon on the Beatitudes, the site of his transformation, and the hill of his crucifixion.

Some of the mountain imagery of Scriptures might have been transposed by the Irish saints to places such as Croagh Patrick and Brandon, but the mountains of the Old and New Testaments are generally mere hills compared to the summits of Connemara and Kerry. Scriptures notwithstanding, throughout most of Europe's Christian era, high peaks were places to be feared—dark, stormy, and forbidding, visited only when necessary. Or visited, perhaps, precisely because one wished to encounter the source of one's fear. Patrick and Brendan took their forty days and forty nights of Christlike solitude in places that less God-mad persons would stay away from.

Of course, external threats of one sort or another could make the mountains places of necessary refuge. High on the eastern side of Brandon, above the Faha pilgrim path in a place seldom visited by climbers, is the collapsed remnant of one of Ireland's most impressive promontory forts of the late Bronze Age or early Iron Age (about 500 B.C.), a pair of massive stone walls guarding the sole approach to an otherwise inaccessible shoulder of the mountain. To this formidable redoubt a pastoral people might have retreated with their animals and goods in times of troubles, presumably in hope that no enemy would be brave enough to follow. It is a grim, cloud-shrouded place, with precipitous slopes on three sides. No one would live there who had not made the choice under dire duress, but duress of one sort or another has driven the Irish into the mountains throughout their history. In every craggy nook of the Kerry mountains can be found ruined hovels that once housed families driven from better circumstances by land seizures, evictions, or religious persecution. The language, religion, and traditions of the people were kept alive in these inhospitable places. Every mountain valley of Kerry has its traditional "Mass stone," where priests are said to have celebrated the Eucharist when it was forbidden by the invader's law. Common Irish place names such as Knockanaffrin (Mountain of the Mass) recall those times.

The literary critic Marjorie Hope Nicholson has shown how mountains were long shunned by Europeans as "tumors," "wens," and "blisters" on the landscape, wretched disfigurements of nature that threatened the beauty of the Earth. The idea that one might go to the mountains for aesthetic delight was simply not entertained by common folk, at least not in the European tradition considered by Nicholson. Some medieval writers even suggested that mountains were not part of the original creation but were a consequence of the Original Sin, or of Cain's transgression, or (since mountains are not mentioned in the Bible before the story of Noah) part of God's plan to punish the Earth by flood.

It does appear that Patrick and Brendan took themselves willingly to summits. There is no way of knowing the motives of those holy men. We must suppose that they found some sort of satisfaction—aesthetic or penitential—in the raging wind and sheeting rain, the cold and solitude. The few surviving written works from their time describe a God who is immanent in nature to an extent that might have been considered heretical on the Continent. It therefore seems likely that early Christian monks of Ireland went to mountaintops for the same reason they established monasteries on craggy cliffs and offshore islands: to open their hearts and minds to a God who spoke through the elements. In this, they set themselves apart from most of their medieval European contemporaries, who generally avoided the mountains as places corrupt and satanic.

Then, according to Nicholson, within a few generations near the end of the eighteenth century, "mountain gloom" gave way to "mountain glory." Poets and philosophers began celebrating high peaks as places of grandeur. Climbers attempted summits in search of the aesthetic sublime. No longer feared, mountains henceforth inspired reverence and exhilaration. Danger, yes, but reward too. Summiting a high peak evoked feelings of pride and satisfaction. Mountaineering was born as a sport and pastime. Wordsworth walked the high ridges of the Lake District "awed, delighted, and amazed," and Byron referred to the Alps as "palaces of Nature"—gathered round their icy summits he discerned "all that expands the spirit, yet appalls." What happened, of course, was the Enlightenment, with its affirmation of the efficacy of human reason, and the beginning of geology as a science. A new way of experiential knowing replaced Scriptures and tradition as sources of truth. The mountains didn't change; what occurred was a shift of focus from the supernatural to the natural, from ignorant fear to insatiable curiosity, from a world ruled by divine whim to a world that might be understood by the human mind. Faith yielded to reason, miracle to law. Now the mountains drew pilgrims precisely because of their wild grandeur. For the modern trekker to Brandon's summit (with her Vibram soles, Gortex jacket, carbon-fiber hiking stick, and plastic water bottle), even the *likelihood* of raging elements is part of the appeal.

TWO STONES IN A ROADSIDE wall not far from my Irish home bracket the change from mountain gloom to mountain glory. The first stone bears an incised cross:

A little farther along, a second stone has a different sort of marking:

The reason for the inscribed cross is not hard to find. In the field below the road is an early ecclesiastical site known as Kilcolman (the church of Colman), a circular earthen wall, now much decayed, enclosing an area about a third the size of a football field, typical of many such structures on the western tip of the Dingle Peninsula.

Inside the ring are hints of former stone huts, perhaps a tiny church. The most striking artifact to attract the visitor today is a large boulder inscribed with two crosses, one of them in a circle, and an inscription in ogham, a Latin-based early Irish alphabet consisting of groups of one to five slashes carved to either side or across a central line.

The inscription on the Kilcolman stone reads (according to a widely accepted interpretation) "Colman the Pilgrim" and may signify the burial place of an important medieval personage who died here on pilgrimage to the summit of Mount Brandon, a place made holy even then by association with Brendan. (Just south of the Kilcolman enclosure is a holy well dedicated to the saint.) From Kilcolman an ancient track known as the Saint's Road leads past numerous holy places, uphill and down, arriving at last on the summit of the mountain.

The stone in the roadside wall inscribed with a cross was unearthed not long ago by a farmer from a nearby field (where it had perhaps once served as a grave marker), and incorporated into the wall so that the cross is visible to passersby. These days, the only pilgrims likely to come this way are young backpackers following the Dingle Way, a long-distance footpath that passes along our road. In some superficial ways their experience is similar to that of their medieval counterparts—blistered feet, aching muscles, sleeping rough—but certainly what the modern trekkers seek is not the same. Medieval pilgrims presumably subjected themselves to physical hardship in petition for divine favor, or as contrition for their sins in expectation of paradise. The modern hikers look for their reward in the experience of the walk itself.

It is unlikely that many of the modern backpackers take notice of the cross-inscribed stone half hidden in the bracken. They are more likely to notice the marking on the second stone, farther along the road, if for no other reason than that it is so unusual. The strange stool-shaped symbol is known in Irish as *Lapa na circe* (the hen's foot). It is a benchmark (reference point for elevation) placed there by British Ordnance surveyors during the nineteenth-century mapping of Ireland. Attentive walkers can find "hen's feet" all over Ireland, along roads, on the older walls of villages, sometimes carved into the cornerstones of nineteenth-century houses.

Medieval Christians who visited Kilcolman were presumably interested in a supernatural geography; they had their eye on heaven. The nineteenth-century cartographers who carved the hen's foot were attending *this* world. A cultural sea change had occurred in the interval between the cross and the hen's foot, perhaps the most important intellectual revolution in human history: a shift of interest from vertical to horizontal, from supernatural to natural, associated with the seventeenth-century Scientific Revolution and the eighteenth-century Enlightenment. The significance of the change can be appreciated in the survival of the Kilcolman ecclesiastical site and others like it. During the centuries since these ringed enclosures were abandoned as places of habitation, they were never incorporated into fields for agriculture, though every patch of arable land was precious. These sites survived for many generations because they were thought to be inhabited by fairies or spirits of the dead—farmers feared to evoke otherworldly wrath by incorporating the rings into their fields. Nowadays these so-called fairy forts are protected by national statute. In some country parts of Ireland, the change between the two views—magical ground versus archaeological treasure—occurred rather recently, and quickly, within one generation. The Enlightenment arrived in our village virtually overnight: One day, Kilcolman was a "fairy fort"; the next day a protective marker was put up by the Board of Works.

IN RURAL IRELAND TODAY THE fairies have been expelled from their forts—and from the minds of the people. The bridge of the Enlightenment has been crossed even in the more remote villages of the west. The modern pilgrim who achieves the summit of Mount Brandon no longer believes that she is closer to heaven; her attention is more likely fixed (if the day is clear) on the horizontal geography that lies sprawled in a glorious vista around her, reason enough to climb the mountain.

On any reasonably fine summer day, by late morning there will be a dozen cars in the parking area at Faha, at Brandon's foot, where the path up the eastern slopes of the mountain begins. An occasional climber might pause at the Virgin's shrine to say a prayer, but most—English, Germans, Americans, Irish—head directly up the slopes, through marginal agricultural land, until reaching the ridge. There the path slews south and follows a more gentle grade to the valley of the Owenmore River, a series of ascending rockbound bowls, carved by glaciers, each containing a cold, clear lake. Not far from here, at Peddlar's Lake near Connor Pass, nineteenth-century geologists first recognized the reality of the ice ages in northern Europe; the hanging bowl-shaped valleys on Brandon's flank are identical in structure to valleys in the Alps where living glaciers still grind rock to dust. As one follows the pilgrim path into the shadowed valley of the Owenmore River, evidence of the vanished ice is on every side: in great boulders plucked from the shoulders of the mountain and strewn like marbles down the valley; in polished rock marked with glacial scratches; in rubble ridges (moraines) at the lip of each successive water-filled bowl. Before Brendan, before the warriors of Celtic myth, before any human presence in Ireland, these slopes belonged to moving ice. But not until someone dared to imagine that the mountains were once mantled in glaciers did the boulders, scratches, and moraines appear to be anything other than arbitrary elements of God's design. The natural philosophers of the Enlightenment said: Where you see similar effects, assume similar causes. One can observe the effects of ice in the Alps, for example, where glaciers still reside—the transported boulders, the scratches, the moraines; here on Mount Brandon are identical signatures of natural cause.

At the headwall, water trickles from a hundred springs to gather in icy lakes, where even on a summer's day the water is cold enough to raise goosebumps on the skin of any climber brave enough to go for a swim. The Sun's rays do not often penetrate this deep gash in Brandon's bulk. (Only a modest drop in the planet's average temperature would cause the glaciers to return.) Then, up a path where it seems no path could exist. As one ascends the last few feet of headwall, as often as not a gale raging up the seaward side of the mountain will blow one over backward. Alternatively, on a calm day, one might step onto the ridge to encounter a view that might tumble one over backward by its sheer majesty: the seaswept end of the Dingle Peninsula, patched with green fields, bays where fishing boats bob at anchor, the bump of Mount Eagle, the westernmost hill in Europe, and, beyond, the Blasket Islands reaching out into the Western Sea as if struggling to reach the Land of Delight. To the south, rising from the gray Atlantic like a jagged tooth, is the rock of Skellig Michael, where monks of the Middle Ages built their ultimate retreat, a cluster of "beehive" cells of unmortared stone clinging to a sheer precipice. Not even Brendan's hermitage on Brandon's summit could have offered a less comfortable venue for prayer than the hard, black Skellig.

Buffeted by gale or exhilarated by view, the climber now turns south along the ridge, and the mountain's apex is only a ten-minute climb away, with its modern cross, ruined medieval oratory, holy well, cairn of stones, and theodolite pillar of the Irish Ordnance Survey, the national mapping agency—a conjunction of artifacts succinctly representing Brandon's two geographies, one spiritual, one physical. The climbers who cluster here, wrapped in anoraks and gulping from thermoses of hot tea, are sensitive to both geographies. They understand why Saint Brendan might have chosen this place for forty days and nights of prayer. The climbers linger, knowing that by making the ascent they have experienced mountain glory. They agree with the poet Byron:

> *Are not the mountains, waves, and skies, a part*
> *Of me and of my soul, as I of them?*
> *Is not the love of these deep in my heart*
> *With a pure passion?*

Enlightenment scientists made mountains less fearsome by explaining their natural origins; the romantic poets of Wordsworth's and Byron's generation (foes of Enlightenment hubris) resanctified the mountains by hymning their transcendent grandeur.

Enlightenment and romanticism, natural and supernatural, reason and feeling—these are the mental geographies we will encounter on the mountain, and which the early Irish Christians of Brendan's era resolutely lived as one. On the summit of Mount Brandon the two geographies seem curiously consonant. From the ridge the view is clear to the tiny harbor of Brandon Creek, where Brendan is said to have begun his westward voyage in search of paradise. His boat was made of wooden laths and oxskins sealed with the fat of animals. Similar boats still put to sea from Brandon Creek—the traditional black-beetle curraghs of Ireland's western shore—oxskins replaced by canvas, animal fat replaced by tar. From the summit one can just make out the bobbing craft, on the crested waves beyond Brandon Head. Wild peaks, wild waves, wild skies, *a part of me and of my soul*: natural elements made holy by ecstatic encounter.

CLOGHANE
TWILIGHT OF THE GODS

Cloghane Church

IN THE VILLAGE OF CLOGHANE, at the base of Brandon Mountain hard by Brandon Bay, in an old churchyard of gaping tombs, stands the ivy-covered ruin of a medieval church, listed in an early-fourteenth-century Papal Taxation List for the diocese of Ardfert, Saint Brendan's diocese of nearly a millennium earlier. Only three walls of the chancel are roughly preserved. (The tower remnant of a nineteenth-century Protestant church occupies the site of the nave.) It is a haunting place, silent except for sounds of the sea, the wind, and peeping wrens in the ivy. Like most of the peninsula's late-medieval structures, the walls of the church were built of mortared rubble, with dressed stone used only around the windows and doors— sills, jams, and lintels. For many years, perhaps centuries, a carved stone human head projected from high on the south wall, face splotched with lichens, eyes gaping, mouth puckered as if to utter a surprised syllable. The head is considered by archaeologists to date from pagan times, which in this case means before the coming (more properly, return) of Patrick to Ireland in the mid–fifth century. As such, it may be the oldest human likeness in County Kerry. In 1993 the head was stolen, levered from the wall and carried away, leaving a gaping hole like a missing tooth; it has not been recovered.

No one knows for certain when or why the Cloghane stone head was sculpted, or whom it represents, if anyone at all. Whatever its origin, the head is regarded locally as that of the pagan magician and harvest god Crom Dubh (Black Crom), over whom Saint Brendan is said to have achieved a spiritual victory in the name of the Christian religion. Crom Dubh's role in Irish life long predates Brendan's arrival on the scene, and to understand his story we must make a diversion into deep cosmic time.

Four and a half billion years ago the solar system was born in a whirling nebula of gas and dust in an outer arm of the Milky Way Galaxy. The nebula began to contract under the influence of gravity. As the cloud got smaller, it spun faster, as an ice skater spins faster as she draws her arms closer to her body. As the cloud spun faster, it flattened out, like a mass of spinning pizza dough. (Astronomers see similar disks of dust and gas around some other stars, other solar systems aborning.) This whirling pancake of dust and gas became our solar system when gravity had gathered most of the material into spinning globes. By far the greater part of the original material of the nebula was pulled to the center of the nebula to form the Sun, our star. Other eddies within the cloud became planets, and the moons of planets (although not, apparently, the Moon of Earth, which was probably created by a later collision of a Mars-sized object with Earth). There was considerable chaos within the cloud. When the third planet from the Sun finally settled into a permanent orbit, its spin axis had a tilt of twenty-three and a half degrees to the plane of the solar system. It was the luck of the draw. It might have been thirty degrees. It might have been zero. If it was zero, our story would have had another beginning. There would be no Crom Dubh.

As the Earth circumnavigates the Sun, sometimes the planet's northern pole is tipped toward the Sun, sometimes away. In the first instance, the Sun's rays fall more directly upon the surface of the northern hemisphere and heat the land and sea more efficiently. In the latter case, the Sun's rays shine obliquely and spread their energy less efficiently. If there had been no tilt, there would be no seasons. Climate, yes—cold poles and hot equator—but no seasonal variations. Without a tilt, in temperate midnorthern latitudes, where many European cultural traditions had their origin, the weather would have been springlike or autumnlike all year long. Crops might be sown and harvested at any time of the year; newborn lambs might gambol with equal friskiness in March or December. But there *was* a tilt, and the waxing and waning of the Sun's warmth and light was *the central fact of life* for people living away from the tropics. Great festivals were celebrated on the days when the Sun stands highest or lowest in the sky. The bonfires of St. John's Eve, June 23, which are still lit in some parts of Europe, including Ireland, celebrate the Sun's ascension to its highest place in northern skies. Likewise, the winter solstice, when the Sun stands lowest, was marked with feasts of light to ensure the Sun's return. (These ancient pagan rites linger in the Christian feast of Christmas and the Jewish Hanukkah.) The equinoxes, when the Sun is halfway between its extremes of strength and weakness, were celebrated too. The spring equinox retains a place in the Christian calendar through its connection with Easter, or alternatively, in

Ireland, with St. Patrick's Day. Celebrations of the fall equinox have slipped from prominence in modern times, but they too were important in the distant past.

The cross-quarter days, midway between the solstices and equinoxes, are less familiar, but they figured in ancient rites and find their counterparts in our modern traditions. The first cross-quarter day should astronomically fall about February 4 or 5. This became Candlemas Day, February 2, in the Christian calendar. An old European rhyme asserts: "If Candlemas be fair and bright, Come, winter, have another flight. If Candlemas brings clouds and rain, Go, winter, and come not again." Some Europeans looked for the shadow of the hedgehog on Candlemas Day; German immigrants brought the tradition to America and substituted the American woodchuck, or groundhog, for the hedgehog, and so on the first cross-quarter day folks in Punxsutawney, Pennsylvania, now look for the shadow of the famous groundhog Punxsutawney Phil. We celebrate the second cross-quarter day as May Day. The third cross-quarter day, which falls in early August, is remembered in the European calendar as Lammas, or "loaf-mass," a harvest feast, but it has mostly vanished from our attention. The fourth cross-quarter day remains prominently with us as Halloween and All Saints.

All over Ireland, and much of Europe, there are prehistoric tombs and megalithic stone structures aligned to the solstices and equinoxes, most famously at Stonehenge in England. The huge grave complex at Newgrange, north of Dublin, is older than the Egyptian pyramids; at dawn on the winter solstice a ray of the Sun penetrates to the largest tomb's deepest chamber. Elsewhere in Ireland, standing stones and stone circles mark with their alignments the Sun's annual peregrinations. On the hill above my Irish home, not far from Mount Brandon, is a wedge grave of massive stones, known locally as the Giant's Bed, aligned to the Sun's equinoctial rising; I have gone there at dawn on the equinox, stretched myself out on the so-called bed, and watched the Sun's red orb appear between my toes on the eastern horizon. Whatever ancient chieftain was buried there knew his promise of resurrection was somehow linked to the daily and yearly passages of the Sun across the sky—into cold and darkness, then back again to light and warmth. The Sun's journey was the astronomical archetype for the voyage of Bran to the Land of the Women and the other westerning excursions recounted in Irish myths.

Clearly, the religion of these prehistoric peoples was predominantly Sun-centered, as might be expected in latitudes where light and life depended utterly upon the twenty-three-and-a-half-degree tilt of the planet's axis. In our more technological times, in the developed world at least, the Earth's nod toward or away from the Sun is mostly a matter of variable leisure activities—put away the golf clubs, bring out the skis—but thousands of years ago *everything* depended upon crops and animals whose flourishing ensured the survival of the tribe. The farther north one travels from tropic climes, the more prominent are the solar variations—in temperature, in the length of the growing season, in the respective hours of daylight and darkness. At the latitude of Mount Brandon, about fifty-one degrees north of the equator, the light barely fades from the northern horizon at high summer, and winter nights are long and dreary, enough reason to attend with fear and hopefulness, petition and thanksgiving, the comings and goings of the Sun.

ELECTRIC LIGHTS AND A READY supply of gas or oil for domestic heating make attention to the Sun's diurnal and annual cycles materially redundant for many of us in the developed world today. Our bodies, however, bear natural clocks that were set in their running during our species' long evolution as hunter-gatherers. For all of our technological sophistication, the Sun retains its hold on our bodily rhythms.

If experimental animals are kept under conditions of constant light and temperature, their internal clocks keep ticking, with circadian (circa-dian, "roughly daily") and circannual ("roughly annual") rhythms. Anyone who has suffered jet lag knows that humans are not exempt from biological timekeeping. After a flight from the United States to Ireland, for example, my internal clock keeps running on the old time, and several weeks will pass before it comes into sync with my new environment. Mosquitoes, morning glories, even bread molds possess circadian rhythms; only the most primitive single-cell organisms appear to be without internal timekeepers. The mimosa plant was one of the first organisms to reveal innate timekeeping. In the 1700s, French scientists maintained mimosa plants under conditions of constant light and discovered that the leaves continued to open and close at approximately daily intervals—with a period of about twenty-two hours (the "roughly daily") instead of twenty-four hours. Without adjustment by exposure to a natural rhythm of day and night, the mimosa's clock runs somewhat fast.

What are these internal clocks, where are they located, and what makes them tick? Something wakes me from deep sleep at approximately the same time every morning, almost to the minute, but what? Hamsters are perfect experimental animals for biorhythm research because their wheel-running activity, which normally takes place at night, is easily monitored. Hamsters continue to take their daily run on a wheel even if kept in constant light. It is thought that the hamster's clock—and those of other mammals—lies in that part of the brain called the suprachiasmatic nuclei (SCN). In the absence of external stimuli, the free-running rhythm of hamster circadian clocks is never less than twenty-three and a half hours. Well, almost never. One researcher found a mutant hamster with a twenty-two-hour circadian clock, from which he derived a line of short-rhythm offspring. He showed that he could shorten the rhythm of wheel-running activities in normal hamsters by surgically excising their SCN and inserting SCN from fetal mutants—twenty-four-hour hamsters turned into twenty-two-hour hamsters by SCN transplants. A more convincing demonstration of the location of the mammalian circadian clock could hardly be imagined. There is still much to be done in figuring out what it is that "ticks" and how it ticks. Locating the gene or genes that control circadian rhythms will help researchers find the answers. Suffice it to say, we share with hamsters biological clocks whose rate of running is genetic. Our bodies are timepieces set by the Sun.

So even if we engineer ourselves away from dependence on solar heat and light, the Sun maintains a claim on human history through the agency of our genes. This may partly account for our enduring fascination with the ancient myths and religious practices of all cultures, which are often based on solar cycles, and with megalithic monuments such as Stonehenge or Newgrange that give the Sun's eternal return physical embodiment. Even the little fragment of medieval church at Cloghane is aligned pretty nearly to an east-west axis, almost certainly by design rather than accident.

NOT FAR AWAY FROM CLOGHANE'S medieval church, in the townland of Cloonsharragh, is a remarkable row of standing stones aligned with the rising Sun on the morning of the summer solstice. Three stones standing taller than a man march up a slight incline toward the northeast. Two other stones have fallen and are now partly buried. A considerable effort must have been involved in dragging these sandstone giants from their place of origin and heaving them into verticality. The date of the construction is not certain, but the alignment seems to belong to the Bronze Age, sometime between 1400 and 700 B.C., certainly before the coming of the Celts to Ireland. The place retains to this day an aura of prehistoric mystery. We cannot, of course, enter into the minds of the people who raised the stones, but we can be sure that awareness of the solar cycles was at the center of their lives.

Remarkably, although the thoughts of Bronze Age Irish are entirely lost to us, it is possible to reconstruct with precision what they saw in the sky. The tradition of precise solar observations, begun in prehistoric times and represented by the Cloonsharragh stone alignment, has led in the fullness of time to the wonders of mathematical astronomy. Using software called Starry Night Pro, I am able to display on the screen of my computer an exact representation of the sky—Sun, Moon, stars, and planets—on any date in the past or future, at any place on Earth. I can transport myself, for instance, to the Cloonsharragh alignment in the predawn hours of the summer solstice in, say, the year 700 B.C. In my imagination, I stand there with others of my tribe, dressed in skins and bronze ornaments, eager, expectant. There is a chill in the air. During the night, the Moon, Jupiter, and Saturn have slipped to their western setting behind the black bulk of Mount Brandon. Now Venus blazes low in the northeast, out across the silver sheet of Brandon Bay. (What names these places had then we'll never know.) The sky glows violet, pink, yellow. Mars, we know, is there in the Sun's glow, hidden. Then, just at the place indicated by the row of standing stones—those dragon teeth!—the Sun explodes above the horizon, glorious, golden, flooding the sea and land with liquid bronze. The year has reached its apex. Our lives are delivered the balm of warmth and light. The gods have heard our petitions and honored them. Again.

THE STONE ALIGNMENTS AND CIRCLES of the British Isles are pre-Celtic. By the time the Cloghane church was built, two thousand years after the Cloonsharragh alignment, continental Europeans were raising magnificent cathedrals aligned on a vertical axis, soaring heavenward with vaults and buttresses. The pre-Christian Celts of Ireland did not, insofar as we know, build temples or churches. A forest grove or the land around a wooded pool was a satisfactory venue for their religious observances. There is undoubtedly a symbolic significance to the places people choose to worship their gods. The astronomically aligned stone circles of the Bronze Age, such as Stonehenge, were designed to be looked *out of,* at the horizon, and to mark the risings and settings of the Sun. The Gothic cathedrals of medieval Europe focus one's attention upward; the stained-glass windows of the cathedrals let in light dappled with scenes from the lives of Christ, the Virgin, or saints, but they are otherwise opaque to the world of nature. The druidic Celts, by contrast, seem not to have felt the need for walls or stone screens to define their sacred places. An oak wood, a forest pool—these suggested sufficient mystery to inspire their sacred rituals, which (lest we become *too* romantic) might have included the occasional human sacrifice.

Among the pagan Celts of Ireland, the most important religious festivals seem to have been associated with the solar cross-days, halfway between the equinoxes and solstices. Imbolc, in early February, is the Celtic equivalent of Groundhog Day; Bealtaine is the Celtic May Day; Lughnasa, near the first of August, is the cross-day that has mostly been forgotten, although not in the west of Ireland (it came to international prominence lately in the title of an award-winning play by the Donegal playwright Brian Friel, *Dancing at Lughnasa*); and Samain, in early November, corresponds to our Halloween, All Saints' Day and All Souls' Day.

Samain and Bealtaine divided the year into a cold season and a warm season, the end and the beginning of grazing. Celtic Ireland's economy revolved first and foremost about cattle, as evidenced by the prevalence of cattle in Irish legends. At Samain, as winter approached, animals not needed for breeding the following year were slaughtered. (The saving of hay as winter feed for cattle was unknown in Ireland until relatively recent times.) One can imagine the feasting that ensued, the heady smell of roasting animal flesh, the fingers sticky with blackened fat and marrow. Drink, too, must have been much in evidence—music—dance—a final glorious debauch before the Sun glided into its southern minimal arc and darkness and cold descended. Samain feasters felt the near proximity of their departed dead, and on the eve of the festival (our Halloween) ghostly spirits were presumed to roam the surrounding hills and fields. It was a time of tricks and treats, of mischievous magical presences and full bellies. Sacrifices were offered to ensure the Sun's return. The members of an extended tribe gathered at Samain one last time before dispersing to their separate places of winter hibernation.

Then, winter not yet past, came Imbolc, the next of the cross-days, on February 1. Days grew noticeably longer, winter's back was broken, and people suffering from claustrophobia and Sun deprivation could certainly have used some cheering up. Little is known of how the festival of Imbolc was observed before the coming of Christianity. The day is now the feast of Saint Brigit, an early Irish saint whose story is richly embroidered with pagan associations carried by the Celts on their long migration from central Europe to the Atlantic fringe.

Bealtaine, May 1, welcomed the Sun's return, the season of warmth and new pasturage. The name of the festival may mean "bright fire." It celebrated the god Belenus, whose name also evokes fire, and whose ancient cult left residues of worship all along the paths of Celtic migration, in northern Italy and southeastern Gaul, for example. Even in modern times bonfires are sometimes lit on May Day in Ireland.

It is the fourth of the cross-day festivals that most concerns us here: Lughnasa, the "feast of Lug," a pagan god. The little ruined medieval church at Cloghane near Brandon's foot remains today the site of Lug's Christianized ritual. He was a favored deity of the Celts—bright, young, fleet-footed, long-armed, and many-gifted—who gave his name to several European places of habitation as the Celts passed through on their westward migration: Leiden in Holland and Lyon in France, for example, supposedly incorporate the etymology of the dashing god. The Irish historian Máire MacNeill found nearly two hundred places in Ireland where Lug's ancient rites were celebrated into recent times, overlaid, of course, with Christian ritual and meaning. According to MacNeill, the original festival was celebrated by the first cutting of the corn. An offering was made to Lug by carrying the corn to a high place and burying it; a bull was sacrificed; a stone head of Lug's archrival Crom Dubh, Black Crom, the god who begrudgingly controls the solar bounty, was installed on a hilltop and triumphed over by an actor impersonating Lug; then followed three days of merrymaking, food and drink, presided over by the human representative of the bright young god; finally, a special ceremony confirmed that Crom Dubh's power was broken, and Lug returned to his rightful place. The time of harvest was full and complete.

Today's Puck Fair in Killorglin, County Kerry, in late summer, a remnant of the festival of Lug, is still wonderfully pagan in its traditions, and the "pattern" (religious procession and ritual) at Cloghane on the last Sunday in July, Domhnach Crom Dubh (Crom Dubh Sunday), was another. The festivities at Cloghane began on the Sunday morning with a climb of Mount Brandon from the east at Faha or from the west at Ballybrack. After religious ceremonies at the summit site of Brendan's hermitage, all of the pilgrims descended the steep eastern path for a visit to the ruined medieval church and the nearby Saint Brendan's holy well. The pattern at Cloghane involved multiple perambulations of both church and well, accompanied by appropriate prayers, all of this observed by the gaping eyes of Crom Dubh, installed during all of those years of pious devotion in the church's interior wall, imprisoned there, one supposes, by the new Lug—Christ, Light of the World.

If Christ was the new Lug, then in Ireland Patrick was his human representative, and it is Patrick who in most places is credited with finally banishing Crom Dubh. In Kerry legend, Lug's role is assumed by Brendan, and Crom Dubh is remembered as a local pagan chieftain who is converted to Christianity by Brendan with the help of a bull. Máire MacNeill collected many stories of Brendan and Crom Dubh near the base of Mount Brandon. A common version goes something like this:

> *Brendan and his brethren are erecting a church at Cloghane. They ask the local pagan chieftain, Crom Dubh, for a contribution. He volunteers a bull, knowing full well that the bull is wild and dangerous. When the monks lead the bull placidly away, Crom Dubh furiously demands the animal's return. Brendan writes the words* Ave Maria *on a piece of paper and suggests to Crom Dubh that the paper*

weighs more than the bull. Nonsense, asserts the pagan chieftain. A scale is arranged, and, sure enough, the slip of paper outweighs the bull. Crom Dubh is so impressed by this apparent miracle that he submits to conversion, and an effigy of his countenance is installed in the church.

Thus did Brendan confound his dark adversary; thus does the power of storytelling clothe the new faith with the raiment of the old. Central to the story, of course, is the power of written language, which Brendan and his fellow monks introduced to Ireland.

LUG AND CROM DUBH WERE deities of a pastoral people, a people whose lives were intimately connected with the cycles of the Sun—light and dark, heat and cold, good and evil, life and death—a people whose well-being rested precariously upon the fulcrum of the seasons. The gods of the pre-Christian Celts were gods of diurnal and annual polarities, of battle and strife, of sexuality and fecundity. The many Celtic myths still so lovingly recounted in Ireland are stories of gods and humans who intermix freely, and indeed who are sometimes indistinguishable; stories of heroes and heroines, cattle, fish, birds, and strong steeds; stories of passionate love affairs, elopements, abductions, and the clash of arms. The Celts carried these stories with them on their long migrations across Europe, until they reached the Atlantic shore and could go no farther. Here, against the barrier of the sea, the new religion of Christianity caught up with them, collided really, two great ways of organizing and making sense of experience, crushed together in Ireland and forced to accommodation.

As one might expect of a religion that had its origin in a place where seasonal variations in light and darkness are less dramatic, Christianity is only loosely linked to solar cycles, and then only by appropriation of older pagan forms. It is by and large a faith of city residents—of shoemakers, tax collectors, tally clerks, potters, tailors, weavers, bakers, professional soldiers, surveyors—a faith that could only have had its origin in the settled civilizations of the Near East, and only flourished in the temperate latitudes of the Mediterranean basin and within the political orbit of the Pax Romana. Unlike Celtic paganism, in which light and dark, order and chaos contend in the world with equal force, Christianity raises light and order to a position of supremacy; darkness and disorder are lesser forces, always with us, to be sure, like a nattering toothache, but destined to yield to the Light of the World. The Christian deity is supremely aloof to the comings and goings of the Sun, sweating beasts and growing plants, sex and procreation. The God of orthodox Christianity enters the world in the guise of his desexualized Son (consider the universal androgynous image), the offspring of a virgin, and then only temporarily. His message is clear: The world of nature is a base and fallen place, to be abandoned as soon as possible for the transcendent and immaterial advantages of heaven. *All flesh is grass and its glory is like the wild flower's; the grass withers, the flower falls, but the word of the Lord remains forever:* the word of the Lord, the writing on the slip of paper that confounds the power of natural fecundity.

Certainly, prominent elements of Christian faith—incarnation, transubstantiation, resurrection of the body, the liturgical year and canonical hours—speak to the *embeddedness* of spirit in matter, perhaps more strongly in the Catholic than the Protestant tradition, but my own religious education turned one's attention away from the world of the senses toward things ethereal and eternal. Our liturgical lives may have been wedded to bread and wine, fire and water, smoke and wax, but those elemental contingencies were understood to be mere stepping stones for our immortal souls on their way to the mysterious and immaterial Beatific Vision. The important thing was not the *patterns* of nature but the *interruptions* of pattern, the miracles that were the signatures of God's *separateness* from creation (not least, the singular miracle of Christian faith, Christ's rising from the dead). Western culture's long quest to weigh the respective claims of natural and supernatural, matter and spirit, tipped in the historical Christianity of my childhood toward supernatural and spirit in ways that (as I would later learn) do not sit comfortably with a modern scientific understanding of the world.

The Romans with their multitude of randy, busybody, quarreling gods—tribal gods, city gods, *household* gods— saw only superstition in the otherworldly preoccupations of the monotheistic Christians, a people who willingly courted martyrdom, enthusiastically embracing severance from the world of the senses. But, of course, Christianity was the perfect religion for an empire, as Constantine astutely recognized when he converted to the new faith in A.D. 312, taking the Roman Empire with him. What better faith for an empire than one that combines all effective power in a single omnipotent deity? What better faith for an empire than one that asks its adherents to meekly turn the other cheek, to render unto

Caesar that which is Caesar's? As Constantine and succeeding Christian emperors consolidated their temporal power, missionaries were dispatched to the farthest reaches of Roman influence. Patrick reached Ireland in the mid–fifth century, but there may have been a tentative Christian presence in the south of the island even earlier. Imperial Rome withdrew its armies from Britain in 410, and within a century Roman political hegemony in Europe collapsed under relentless "barbarian" pressure from outside and a softness at the center, but the spiritual hegemony of Christianity survived and grew stronger. The all-powerful godhead was now embodied in the papacy, and soon enough the pagan tribes were converted to Christ.

All of Europe sent their tithes to the Roman church, even as the political empire shattered. Sometime in the early sixth century, Brendan had his legendary encounter with Crom Dubh at the foot of Mount Brandon in the west of Ireland, and the Light of the World cast his beam into this remote corner of Europe's Atlantic fringe. A stone head that until recently was stuck up on the chancel wall of a ruined thirteenth-century church is all that remains (wherever it is currently hidden) of the pagan forces of nature that annually did battle with Lug for earthly dominion. Once Roman Christianity had consolidated its influence in Ireland, which required several centuries after the time of Patrick and Brendan, the Sun no longer needed to be coerced to remit its bounty; by then the welfare of the people was in the care of a God who exists outside of nature, and for whom the Sun, as all of nature's benefices or devastations, is given or withheld at whim. "'Tis a fine soft day, thanks be to God," the Irish say. Whatever happens in the world is the result of a constantly renewed contract between the people and the transcendent deity who rules the world; unruly nature has nothing to do with it.

But for a brief and extraordinary time after the fifth-century collision of Christianity with Irish paganism something rather different emerged, an amalgam faith embracing elements of the ethereal monotheism of the citified eastern Mediterranean and the earthy polytheism of the pastoral Celts. All the world is a story, the early Irish saint Colum Cille supposedly said, and, if so, wisely. There was something about the Celtic gift of storytelling that gave Irish Christianity its unique character. From what we can tell, the peoples of the Atlantic fringe had a history of using language to conjoin apparent opposites. They were (and are) masters of the double meaning, the pun, the riddle, the thing that is neither this nor that but both, the thing that is this *and* that but neither. We find residues of this fondness for ambiguity in some of the Celtic traditions that survived into modern times. The dew of May Day dawn, for example, comes from neither earth nor sky, exists on the cusp of night and day, and belongs to neither winter nor summer; it is from this suspension betwixt and between that the prophylactic efficacy of May Day dew derives in the old tradition. Mistletoe is neither shrub nor tree, and does not grow from the ground like other plants; it defies the usual classifications and thereby escapes the limitations of definitions, and so by standing under mistletoe one is likewise exempt from the usual strictures that would prohibit, say, a lad kissing a lass. Irish myths are full of narrow doors, slender threads, and delicately balanced fulcrums by

which one escapes the usual clash of opposites and para-
doxes of reason. The gods of the Celts were not quite
human and not quite divine, but both. The Celtic otherworld is almost other but not quite; return might just be
possible by magic (but take care not to set your foot on the
ground); time spent in the otherworld is both longer and
shorter than ordinary time. And most especially, the Irish
poets deemed the seashore the place where *éicse*—wisdom, poetry, knowledge—is revealed, neither land nor
sea, neither this world nor the other, as befits a people
who lived pressed up against an apparently limitless
expanse of water, jostled from behind by reason, beck-
oned before by mystery. When faced with a conflict
between continental Christianity and the faith of their
druidic ancestors, the Irish employed their native genius
for finding the thing that is neither but both, and forged
a faith that for several centuries energized an astonishing
species of Celtic Christian culture, which—as I hope to
show—has relevance for resolving the *this or that* dilemmas of our own time.

But before we leave the little ruined church at Cloghane and begin our climb up the mountain, there is one
last association that might be mentioned. If the stone head
formerly lodged in the chancel wall is indeed a pagan artifact, as the archaeologists say, it is one of only a few such
pre-Christian idols that have survived in southwest Ireland. It served into modern times as a cult object for the
cure of toothache—old necromancer Crom Dubh's magical power invoked to allay the most human of maladies,
the most nettlesome of pains. If there is anything that truly
separates us from our ancestors, pagan or early Christian,
it is toothache—in their time an all-pervasive, lifelong

scourge, seldom life threatening, but guaranteed to make life miserable for rich or poor, king or peasant. As I stand within the ivy-covered walls of the ruined Cloghane church, where the head of Crom Dubh until recently presided and where I examined his countenance when I first came to Ireland, I know that it is not the old gods of the pagan Celts nor the newer God of Mediterranean Christianity that have given me a life mostly free of the scourge of toothache, but science, a way of organizing experience that assumes all things happen by natural cause—such as the bacterial origins of toothache, or the cycles of the Sun and Moon, which keep their appointed rounds no matter whether or not we observe prescribed rituals. The theft of the stone head from Cloghane church is an archaeological misfortune, but no great loss to the people of Cloghane. It is not to a talisman they turn today when they suffer toothache, but to doctor and pharmacist.

3

FAHA
LAND OF MILK & HONEY

ONE MILE UP A TARMACKED track from Cloghane village, at the five-hundred-foot elevation above sea level and with stunning views across Brandon Bay (when the tide is out, a broad expanse of sand) is the tiny community of Faha, a handful of farmsteads on marginal land, a last faint hold on lowland fertility before the blanket bog. This is the traditional beginning place for the eastern ascent of Brandon, for the religiously motivated pilgrims who have made the trek for more than a thousand years, many with bare feet, and for the secular hill walkers who arrive today with sturdy boots and daypacks. Since I first ascended the mountain from here thirty years ago, the Kerry County Council has provided a graveled parking area for half a dozen cars, but on a sunny day in summer as many more again may be jammed into the verges by the side of the road. A large sign provided by the Kerry Mountaineering Club warns climbers that weather conditions on the summit can be wildly different from those at the mountain's base; make sure you have good boots, warm clothing, rain gear, a map, and a compass, the sign warns ominously: "A breeze here can be a strong wind up there." Up a short, fuchsia-shaded boreen (little road), through a gate that hangs lopsidedly on flimsy hinges, and one is on one's way up the slopes, in the footsteps of Lug and Brendan. But first a stop at the Marian shrine, tucked into the hillside and bracketed by firs and pines, where every pious pilgrim said a prayer before attempting the ascent. The Virgin looks down from her central niche, serene, detached, her foot on the Serpent, the two of them perched on the globe of the world. "I am the Immaculate Conception," she supposedly said to Bernadette at Lourdes, and so, for the believing Roman Catholic Christian, God entered the world via the womb of a woman born without the stain of Original Sin.

To the Virgin's left, in a smaller niche, is a statue of Patrick, and to her right is Brendan, boyishly handsome, standing in the boat in which he went in search of the Isles of the Blest. His sculpted portrait, of course, is stylized. We know nothing of what Brendan looked like; indeed, we know very little about him at all with certainty. Most of what we have of the saint—such as the wonder-filled account of his voyage, the *Navigatio Brendani*—was not written down until hundreds of years after his death, when Brendan's own earthy brand of Celtic Irish Christianity had at last succumbed to Mediterranean transcendence.

In the first centuries of the Christian era the art of portraiture in stone had reached a high level of realism in Rome. We know with remarkable fidelity what the long-nosed Emperor Hadrian looked like, for example, and his beautiful curly haired favorite, Antinous. The Romans had a gift for the here and now, *this* particular flesh, *this* particular moment in time. Water, sewerage, roads, granaries—these were their practical imprint on the land. Look at a road map of Britain today, and

Roman practicality is there to see in the arrow-straight modern roads built atop Roman bases that radiate like spokes of a wheel from towns and cities that once were Roman camps. This was a people who appreciated that a straight line is the shortest distance between two points, that time is money, and that money is everything. The wealthy Roman patrician who commissioned his portrait in stone wanted a *recognizable* image, every dimpled chin and bushy brow; there might be in that gentleman's household a stylized image of a god, the Lar of the house perhaps, but the marble bust of the master left no doubt about who *really* ruled the roost. No such representational art then existed on the Atlantic fringes of northern Europe. Life in western Ireland was an altogether dicier thing: pastoral, windblown, god-ridden, precarious. The crude stone head of Crom Dubh that once adorned the wall of Cloghane church is about as close as the pagan Celts came to a realistic portrayal of the human face.

Likewise, we have shelves of written texts from the Romans—history, biography, autobiography, poetry, prose, natural history, philosophy, many times transcribed of course—but hardly anything in written language from Ireland before the time of Patrick. Ogham script had taken hold in southwestern Ireland by Brendan's time, but it was suitable only for short memorial inscriptions on stone, not for extended written expositions. Saint Patrick's own compositions (or those purportedly from his hand) are the earliest extant Irish works in Latin. He was born, according to tradition, in Roman Britain, somewhere "between the Rivers Clyde and Severn," about A.D. 390, the son of a Christian Romano-British official named Calpornius, and almost certainly learned to write as a child. According to a common telling (very little is known as historical fact), the boy was abducted at age fifteen, with his sister, by an Irish raiding party led by the famed warlord Niall NaoiGhiallach, Niall of the Nine Hostages, and taken to Ireland as a slave. There he worked as a shepherd or swineherd until, in his early twenties, he escaped his masters and fled to Gaul. His resolve to return someday to Ireland was unflagging, and after many adventures on the Continent and considerable further education, he did return, in middle age, as a consecrated priest of the Roman Church.

The story is as various as the tellers, but all of the sources agree that Patrick's fervor and erudition impressed the pagan Irish lords, confounded the druid priests, and brought the island to Christ. At Kilmalkedar, near the western foot of Mount Brandon, there is a wonderful artifact that dates from perhaps the sixth century—within a century or so of Patrick's arrival in Ireland—a cross-inscribed standing stone, like many to be found within early Irish ecclesiastical sites, but this one with a Latin alphabet inscribed along its spine. It was likely intended for the instruction of local youths in the Latin language, another of many invasions of Ireland, this one of letters rather than of arms, and perhaps the most influential invasion of them all (remember that weighty slip of paper with the words *Ave Maria* by which Brendan confounded Crom Dubh). Only when the Latin alphabet was at their command did the Irish begin to write down the myths and legends of their pagan past, and the remembered lives and teachings of their Christian saints. The Irish took to written language like ducks to water, and in the centuries immediately following their conversion to Christianity became the most scholarly people in western Europe, absorbing whatever works of classical antiquity they could lay their hands on, and soon, reversing Patrick's course, carried their erudition back to the Continent, founding monasteries and centers of learning all across Europe.

IN THE WILD REGIONS AROUND Mount Brandon, Brendan, not Patrick, is remembered best for his physical and spiritual exploits. It was Brendan (in local legend) who won this isolated corner of Ireland to Christ. It was Brendan who established a monastic settlement at Shanakeel on the westward flank of Brandon, and perhaps also at the nearby isolated shelf of cliff known as Fothar na Manaigh (the green fields of the monk), a place difficult to access even today. (I have scrambled down there several times, half walking, half tumbling down a pathless slope; there are walled fields and ruined huts of indeterminate age, but nothing that would confirm the presence of the saint.) It was Brendan who retreated in prayerful isolation to the mountain's summit in preparation for his voyage across the sea.

He was born not far from here, near the present town of Tralee, only a generation after Patrick's return to Ireland, to Christian parents who seem to have had some stature in the community, perhaps even drops of royal blood. Tradition gives his father the combined names of Fionn and Lug, two manifestations of the same pagan deity, presumably to emphasize Brendan's role as natural successor to the ancient heroes. The infant boy was baptized by Bishop Erc, whom Patrick had himself baptized at the royal court of Tara. At the age of one year, Brendan was put out to fosterage with a woman named Ita, who ran a school at Ceall Ide, now Killeady in County Limerick. (The girls boarding school in Dingle today is called Colaiste Ide, Saint Ita's College.) Fosterage of a firstborn son was an ancient Celtic custom that survived the island's conversion to Christianity, although by then it was expected of Christian parents that a fostered eldest son would be given to the church for ordination. In any case, Ita was by all accounts a remarkable woman, who took (in the later miraculous tales that enveloped all Irish saints) the infant Jesus to her breast. She taught Brendan to cultivate a pure heart, the simple life, and Christian charity, and to despise a scowling face, obstinacy, and too much money. Of course, we know nothing of what Ita *actually* taught Brendan, if she taught him anything at all, but her supposed curriculum suggests a certain continuity of moral wisdom across the ages. At age six Brendan returned to Kerry, where he continued his education, undoubtedly becoming literate in Latin. Later, he wandered Ireland in search of his spiritual calling, before ordination as a priest in his midtwenties. He soon gathered other men of similar temperament about him and founded monasteries, most especially the famous foundation at Clonfert in County Galway.

As we listen to this recital of royal seats, episcopal palaces and monasteries, it is best not to let images from the later Middle Ages obtain a hold on our imaginations. The Tara of Brendan's time was a typical Iron Age hilltop fort, with earthen banks and buildings that would not pass for much more than hovels today. The countryside around Mount Brandon is dotted with similar, although smaller, "ring forts" (as is much of Ireland), most of which probably had no defensive purpose except against marauding wolves. The largest and most impressive of these so-called forts were ecclesiastical settlements. Not far from Mount Brandon is the well-studied site at Reask, which may have been visited by Brendan. Charcoal from an excavated hearth at Reask yielded a radiological date of A.D. 385 ± 90, which is just about the time of Patrick's birth if we take the mean figure, so the settlement may have been pagan before it was Christian. But Christian it certainly became, for cross-inscribed pillars and slabs have been found there, including one of the most beautifully decorated cross slabs in all of Ireland. Within the confines of a roughly circular wall are the remnants of a tiny oratory, or chapel, and half a dozen circular "beehive" huts, the largest about twenty feet in diameter, which were likely roofed with corbeled stone and thatch. How many people lived at Reask is unknown, but they were surely crowded in their cold, damp, windowless huts. Monastic settlements of Brendan's time were nothing like the images we have of later medieval monasteries, with their soaring chapels and elegant cloisters. The men and women who lived at places like Reask, and who were perhaps better off than most of the locals, did a lot of hunkering and squatting. Where and if they bathed are questions left unanswered by the archaeologist's excavations.

In other words, when Christianity finally pushed Celtic paganism up against the sea and overwhelmed it, the transformation of Irish culture was more intellectual than physical. Folks still lived in the same sorts of houses, wrested a precarious living from the same wild sea and stony soil, told the same stories, played the same music, hunted the same animals. But all of this was by then overlain with a layer of theological abstraction that had swept up into the blustery north from the sunny Mediterranean, still redolent with the scents of cedar and orange blossoms, Greek learning, and Egyptian mysticism. And for a brief time—a few centuries—what resulted might be called "the best of both worlds," a curious brand of Judeo-Christian monotheism that was thoroughly rooted in earth, stone, wind, and wave, that looked not so much eastward toward Jerusalem as westward into the wild, dark sea.

THE SEA! IT BEATS AGAINST the Irish shore, the black cliffs that plunge into the foaming breakers, the seaweedy sand. Irish weather comes from the sea, balmy rains on a southwest wind, icy winds from the north; almost never does the weather on the Dingle Peninsula blow from the east. By contrast, the stars rise in the east, with Sun and Moon, but they go westward. Sun, Moon, and planets swing low across the southern sky, more often than not hidden by cloud, then fall into gray water out there beyond the jagged tooth of the Tearaght Rock, westernmost of the Blasket Islands, where today a winking lighthouse announces Europe to ships coming from America.

Southwestern Ireland's weather is mild because of the prevailing west and southwest winds; wet and sometimes ferociously wild, but always warm. Frosts are rare in Kerry; palm trees and other tropical plants flourish; fuchsia, a fairly modern warmth-loving import from South

America, runs riot in the hedgerows. Plants grow on this shore that are typical of southwestern or southern Europe, the so-called Lusitanian element of Ireland's flora. (Lusitania was the Roman name for the warmer lands of northern Spain and the Pyrenees.) Irish spleenwort, Kerry lily, Saint Patrick's cabbage, and kidney saxifrage are examples of Kerry plants that seem strangely alien. (How Saint Patrick's cabbage got its name is something of a mystery. It is not a cabbage and, as far as I know, has no connection with the saint.) The latter two plants are familiar on the slopes of Brandon, in warm, damp microclimates under overhanging boulders or in cracks in the cliff face, with other delicate beauties like golden saxifrage, maidenhair fern, and dog violet. To the Lusitanian plants can be added a few animals more typical of southern climes than to this northern shore: the gloriously dappled Kerry spotted slug and the warty natterjack toad. How these plants and animals got to Ireland is an unsolved mystery of Irish natural history, but they seem to find the island's southwestern coast congenial. The climate *is* oddly mild for a place at the latitude of icy Labrador, and it seems to have been that way for at least the past several thousand years. Like the Irish today, the pre-Christian people who lived on this rocky rim of Europe kept their backs to winter and looked to the sea for a genial wind. Reason enough, I suppose, to imagine that out there somewhere in that rag-wet sea a place of comfort and rejuvenation might be found.

Gerald of Wales, who wrote a geographic history of Ireland in the twelfth century, commented on the island's felicitous climate. "The most temperate of countries," he called the subject of his treatise. He wrote: "The grass is green in the fields in winter, just the same as in summer. Consequently the meadows are not cut for fodder, nor do they ever build stalls for their beasts. The country enjoys the freshness and mildness of spring almost all year round." There was no doubt where the freshness and mildness (and wetness!) came from: off the moderating sea. To the west of Ireland is a mass of relatively warm water. The air moves across the water, soaking up evaporated moisture, like a paper towel moving across a wet kitchen counter, to wring itself out on Ireland's west coast. The warmer the water, the more readily evaporation feeds moisture into the air, and North Atlantic water is anomalously warm.

Why? The Gulf Stream. At least that's what you always hear. You read it in books, newspapers, tourist brochures. The Gulf Stream laps Kerry's shore, bringing scents of the south and tropic breezes; Mexican heat dragged north by a river in the sea to give Ireland a mild, moist climate. But the truth is rather more complicated. True enough, the rivers in the sea are there. The South Equatorial Current flows across the top of South America into the Caribbean Sea. Four and a half million years ago it passed into the Pacific between North and South America, which were not then connected. Then volcanic activity heaved up the isthmus at Panama (a geologic episode of enormous consequence for Ireland's weather). The South Equatorial Current was deflected northward into the Gulf of Mexico, where it is warmed further like water in a pan, finally escaping between Florida and Cuba to feed the Gulf Stream, an arrow of heat aimed at Kerry. It is not quite clear what happens to all this liquid warmth; somewhere near the Grand Banks of Newfoundland the boundaries of the stream get messy. The Gulf Stream collides with the cold Labrador Current coming down from the north, and dissolves into eddies of curling water. Some of the stream peals off southward to feed the Azores Anticyclone. Some of what's left joins the North Atlantic Drift, stoking the evaporation that douses Dingle.

Geochemist Wallace Broecker has another idea. On the basis of a huge mass of sea data, he proposes a globe-spanning oceanic conveyor belt with its northern terminus near Iceland. Cold winds from Canada blow across the water, cooling it. The cold, dense water sinks, and flows as a deep bottom current southward around Africa's Cape of Good Hope into the Indian and Pacific Oceans. There it rises, warms, and as a shallower current returns to the Atlantic and flows northward. Near Iceland, this water from a tropic sea somehow finds its way to the surface, where its heat is again stolen away by Canadian winds. These are the balmy, moisture-drenched westerlies that warm and wet Ireland. If Broecker is right, Kerry's agreeable breezes have their ultimate source in palm-fringed oceans half a world away.

Of course, the people who lived on this shore two thousand years ago knew nothing of transoceanic geography or deep-sea currents. With arctic cold at their backs and warmth coming from the sea, they must have wondered at the source of those beneficial winds. Undoubtedly, they noticed other strange and wonderful things coming from the west. Birds, for example. Every year Irish ornithologists observe stray North American species, mostly on Ireland's Atlantic-facing shore. The majority of these avian immigrants are shorebirds and waders, strong-flying, long-distance migrants that have been blown or wandered off course from their usual patterns of migration. Rarely, a less far-ranging land species shows up in Ireland: an indigo bunting, bobolink, scarlet tanager, redstart, or American robin, for example. It is almost impossible to imagine how these creatures make an Atlantic crossing of two thousand miles, even with the help of a trailing wind, but somehow they do. They arrive exhausted and confused. Altogether, about 150 species of American birds have been observed in Ireland. We have no idea to what extent the pre-Christian inhabitants of Ireland took note of birds, but it seems unlikely that an exotic visitor, especially of gaudy plumage—a scarlet tanager, perhaps—would have gone unnoticed, or that the prevalence of these visitors on western shores would not have suggested a transoceanic origin. Even North American monarch butterflies have been observed in western Ireland. I sometimes wonder if the occasional colorful and unfamiliar migrant, apparently arriving on westerly winds, might have reinforced in the minds of the early inhabitants of these shores the idea of a place strange and wonderful, a Land of Delight, out there beyond the misty western horizon.

AMERICA WOULD IN DUE TIME become a literal promised land for a subjugated people racked by famine, but in Brendan's day a rather different sort of place was thought to lie out there in the mists: a land of pleasure where saints reign immortal, the Blessed Western Isles. Let Mediterranean Christians look for heaven across the great metaphysical divide of death, and let them court martyrdom to speed the transition; the gulf between heaven and Earth for the early Irish was physical, not metaphysical, and getting there required marine navigational skills, not martyrdom. The otherworld was at hand, somewhere out there in the roiling, fog-blanketed, apparently endless sea. The birds that came to shore—gannets, petrels, shearwaters, terns, and especially the exotic migrants—had to come from somewhere. The waves endlessly rolled shoreward; something set them moving. Where did the Sun go in its setting? For centuries before and after Brendan, the Irish of these rugged shores looked out to sea and wondered. Their stories are full of that wet horizon, and a good example is the tale of Tir na nOg.

The Fianna were Celtic warriors in service to the high king of Ireland during the centuries immediately preceding the coming of Patrick. When the Fianna were not repelling invasions, they spent their time hunting with their dogs and steeds. Once, while hunting near Killarney, they were approached by a beautiful, golden-haired girl, Niamh, on a splendid white charger. She persuaded Oisin, the son of Fionn Mac Cumhail, chief of the Fianna, to come with her to her kingdom beyond the sea. (This tale should have a familiar ring.) They mounted her horse together and thundered toward the Atlantic at Glenbeigh, near the head of Dingle Bay. When they reached the water's edge, the horse took to the air and galloped westward to Tir na nOg, a land of everlasting youth, the place of milk and honey that had long dominated the Irish imagination. After what seemed to Oisin to be a short period of bliss, but which was actually three hundred years, he asked for the opportunity to visit his people. He was given the loan of the flying horse but warned not to set his foot on Irish soil. Oisin flew back across the sea to Ireland and sought the Fianna. Near Dublin, he looked down to see a group of men struggling with a large stone. He leaned from his horse to help them, but the girth broke and he fell to the ground. Immediately, he became an old man, and the horse galloped away.

Oisin's fall from his horse was (or was made so in the retelling) a crucial moment in Irish history. Among the men shifting the stone (in one account) was Patrick, just returned to Ireland on his mission to convert the Irish. Patrick engaged old Oisin in dialogue. The mythical conversation of Christian saint and pagan hero can be taken to stand for a broader and mutually fruitful cultural exchange: The ancient Celtic stories passed into the written language of Christian scribes, whereby they have maintained their hold on the Irish imagination until this day, and the new faith that Patrick brought from continental Europe was transmitted to Oisin's kith and kin. What briefly emerged from the synthesis (represented with such compelling symbolism in the story of Oisin and Patrick) was a curious eschatology in which heaven (or at least a place of prelapsarian bliss) might be reached by earthly endeavor: sailing westward into the Atlantic.

I know of no case of Christian martyrdom in Ireland. The encounter of Christianity and Celtic paganism could not have been without considerable tension, but apparently few Christians died to win passage to paradise. What occurred instead was a melding of two traditions in which the boundary between life and death, and between land and sea, became (for a few centuries) muddled. The dry and sunny monotheism of the eastern Mediterranean became clouded over with the wet polytheism of the Atlantic fringe. The all-embracing earthy gods of the Irish Celts—who might take the form of a horse, bull, hound, wolf, salmon, Sun, male, female— were wedded to the transcendent deity formalized at the Council of Nicaea, who took human form only once in the flesh of his son Jesus Christ. We must suppose that ancient Oisin and Patrick discovered in their purported conversation an improbable affinity, no doubt at least partly because Patrick had spent part of his youth among the pagan Irish. But Oisin too knew something of time and mortality. After all, he had been out there in the Land of Eternal Delight, he had lain for three hundred years in the arms of a golden-haired Niamh, not across a gulf of eternity, not having left his body in the grave, but in living flesh and blood across mere miles of white-crested sea.

SOME ELEMENTS OF OISIN'S STORY—the land of eternal youth, the invitation by a fair maiden—are older and more universal than even the Irish telling. Some sources of Irish myth came all the way from India with the migrations of people more ancient than the Celts. What-ever the sources, it is likely that Brendan, as a boy in Kerry, heard the stories of Bran and of Oisin, and simi-lar tales. As he sat on the shore, at Fenit perhaps, on Tralee Bay, looking out to sea, he might have dreamed of the land of Tir na nOg, all mixed up in his head with the tales of heaven he learned from his Christian teachers. And when the time came, he would put his dreams to the test. He would build himself a boat of wooden laths and oxskins and see for himself exactly what lay out there in the Western Sea.

But wait. Who is this lady standing to Brendan's left in the shrine at Faha, between Brendan and Patrick? With the crown on her head, and her dreamy eyes, and her palms turned outward as if to show that she has nothing to hide? She is dressed in flowing robes from head to toe, with not a hint of décolletage or graceful turn of ankle, the fullness of her breasts disguised by the folds of her mantle. Who is this sexless virgin, mother of God, immaculately conceived? Could this be the fairy lass who invited Bran to sail westward? Is this Oisin's Niamh? Not likely. Few women appear in the stories that have come down to us of Brendan and Patrick, except for the remarkable Ita, Brendan's teacher at Killeady. Were those earliest Irish monks as immune to sexual desire as their stories seem to suggest? It is hard to imagine a more lusty body of lore than the stories of the pre-Christian Irish Celts, so full of wooings and elopements and otherworldly houses with thrice nine maidens and thrice nine beds. And yet, soon upon conversion to Christianity, women seem mostly to disappear from Irish storytelling (except for the ubiquitous Brigit, of whom more anon). Indeed, nothing is more striking about the conversion than the apparent change in attitudes toward women. Lusty adoration became bitter misogyny. One medieval Irish text calls women "greedy," "slanderous," "stingy," and "mischievous." Another, from the ninth century, tells us that

> *The women of the world, except a few,*
> *burn in the fire of Doomsday.*
> *It is not fitting to speak to them*
> *after the murder of John.*

So half the human race gets the blame for Salome's sin, but of course even Salome is blighted with the sin of Eve. When Patrick routed the druid priests, did he banish the attractiveness of women too? By bringing Eve's sin to Ireland did he immediately send the voluptuous fairy princesses scampering for their hills? Somehow, it doesn't seem probable, at least not with such alacrity. We must remember that most of what we know of the earliest Irish Christians was not written down until later, after the Viking invasions of the ninth century and subsequent Norman incursions, when continental Christianity, with its manifest misogyny, had begun to exert its heavy sway over the Irish church and Irish culture. Whenever and however it happened, a dark and misogynistic cloud descended over Ireland, deeply at odds with the Celtic spirit, and not to be removed until our own time.

Of course, tales of pre-Christian Ireland survived in the collective consciousness of the people with a kind of underground existence not unlike that of the fairies themselves, mitigating an oppressive prudery with a faraway, faintly heard fairy music. When nineteenth-century writers and scholars of the so-called Celtic revival rediscovered Oisin and Niamh, and all the other great wooings and elopements of Irish myth (at the same time that mountain gloom gave way to mountain glory), it was as if a sunburst of light broke through the overcast. But even then the fleshy ethic of the Celts was resisted by the Church, confined to pasty storybooks, and bowdlerized. But the force of the stories could not be ultimately resisted. Today, the front tables of every bookshop in Ireland are piled high with illustrated copies of the ancient myths—strapping men, voluptuous women, creatures of flesh and blood, enjoying the carnal pleasures of the elemental world.

Then, there is Brigit, who ranks up there in the Irish pantheon of saints with Patrick, Brendan, and Colum Cille. It would have been unthinkable for the ancient pagan earth goddess, with her ample haunches and pendulous breasts, who left her icons of clay and bone all across pre-Christian Europe, to simply disappear without a trace. On the Continent, the goddess's role was subsumed by Christianity into the cult of Mary, mother of Christ, with lamentable consequences: Fertility was replaced by virginity, robust nakedness by all-concealing robes of chaste white, and equality of male and female divinities by female subservience to a single male God. In Ireland, it was Saint Brigit who took the place of a more ancient fertility goddess of the same name. Imbolc, the pagan cross-day feast of early February, when the fertility of the earth begins to be renewed, is now Saint Brigit's Day. Gerald of Wales, in his thirteenth-century history of Ireland, tells us that the nuns of Kildare—a house founded by Saint Brigit—kept a sacred fire burning in her behalf, not unlike the acolytes of the Roman goddess Vesta. Clearly, the widely venerated Christian saint had her genesis in pagan tradition.

But if Irish reverence for Saint Brigit is a carryover from worship of the earth mother, little of the ancient goddess survived in the newer rites. Saint Brigit became in official church teaching a "second Mary," and her cult became tangled up with that of the mother of Christ. A hymn in honor of Saint Brigit from sometime between the seventh and ninth centuries begins, "Victorious Brigit did not love the world, she perched in it like a bird on a cliff," hardly a description of her pagan namesake, who was awash in the world up to her neck.

Pious pilgrims who ascend Mount Brandon today stop at the Faha shrine to pray to the Virgin and her chaste acolytes, Brendan and Patrick. The three persons depicted by the statues seem ill at ease in their physical bodies, as if waiting to trade them at the first opportunity for pure spirit. The pre-Christian men and women whose traces we will find on the mountain had a far lustier regard for the world of the flesh.

4

BINN NA PORT
THE WILD & THE HOLY

Ruins of fort on the top of Mount Brandon

Λ TYPICAL ASCENT OF MOUNT Brandon from Faha starts in sunshine, but only because I generally wait for a fair day before climbing the mountain. I have learned from long experience that fine weather at the mountain's base does not guarantee clear skies at the top, but at least it makes the first part of the climb more pleasurable. In Ralph Horne's *Geological Guide to the Dingle Peninsula* is reproduced a sketch of Brandon by George Victor Du Noyer, who completed the original mapping of the Dingle Peninsula for the Geological Survey of Ireland in 1856. The sketch shows the mountain from across Smerwick Harbor, its peak wreathed in cloud; "Mount Brandon as usual" is Du Noyer's wry caption. As usual, indeed. Of the nearly one hundred times I have climbed the mountain, I would say the peak has been clear less than a dozen times. On one memorable occasion I climbed with a friend up through clouds to find the tip of the peak under clear blue skies, the clouds held low by an utterly flat temperature inversion. We stood as if on an island in a vast white sea. To the south, also protruding above the sea of cloud, was the summit archipelago of the Macgillicuddy Reeks and Carrantuohill.

The well-worn path from the Faha shrine slants up through rough fields toward a shoulder of the ridge.

This part of the climb is a boring slog, our bodies not yet limbered up and running smoothly. When years ago I guided my children up the mountain, it was along this initial slope that they grumbled most, at the very beginning of the walk when the summit seems infinitely far away and, as often as not, hidden by cloud. But this stretch of the trail is unexciting only if we keep our eyes fixed on the rising path in front of us. If we stop for a minute and turn around, a dazzling prospect spreads before us: the golden sands of Brandon Bay and the hills beyond, including the impressive bulk of Stradbally Mountain and the isthmus of sand connecting the Maharee Islands to the mainland.

At the shoulder of the ridge, the path turns left, the slope becomes less steep, and the climber's spirit improves. The dark corrie of the Owenmore River with its staircase lakes and tumbling waterfalls beckons only a half mile ahead, and once we are there discouragement will sluice away in the beauty of the rough, wild track. But this time we'll not head into the corrie. Instead, we'll leave the path and keep moving straight up the shoulder of the mountain, a climb that gets steeper with every step. Where we are going is a place as remote as any on the peninsula—gloomy, cloud-wrapped, outside of time. Even the archaeologists who did the comprehensive survey of the antiquities of the Dingle Peninsula gave Binn na Port a pass.

Binn na Port, the Peak of the Fort: a jutting promontory of Mount Brandon, like a fist shaken at the world, at an elevation of 2,700 feet above the level of the sea. To the south the promontory falls away into the ice-carved Owenmore corrie; the slope there is strewn with boulders.

To the north is another steep-sided valley, through which the Owennafeana River (the river of the Fianna) flows, but which we call the Airplane Valley because of the many fragments of World War II aircraft that litter the valley floor; five separate planes crashed here during that conflict. To the west, a narrow arête connects the promontory to the main bulk of Brandon mountain. The arête is passable (I have watched others make the traverse), but on two occasions I have turned back from the attempt, dissuaded by slippery footholds bracketed by vertical cliffs. Only from the east is the approach to Binn na Port not fraught with danger—our own approach—and even here it is steep enough. As we near the plateau, we see that this way too is protected; two stone walls bar the approach, stretched defiantly across the promontory's eastern lip from cliff face to cliff face, one behind the other, ten feet thick and, where they are best preserved, as tall as a man.

The Ordnance Survey map labels the structure Dun Cinn Tire, literally "the fort at the head of the country," or simply "promontory fort." It is built of undressed stones laid horizontally, without mortar, some large enough to require the efforts of half a dozen men to wrestle into place. Each of the two walls is pierced with a single gap; it is easy to imagine that timber gates might have once barred the entrances. Hints of terraces can be seen on the inside of both walls, places where warriors might have stood to hurl their spears at besiegers, a sure sign that the walls were defensive in nature. The first wall is longer and is placed across the still-rising slope. A bit more climbing, and you reach the shorter battlement, where the slope narrows. Behind this wall the land flattens out into a sort of mesa, a few acres in extent. On the rare fine day, the views from here in every direction are spectacular.

Once I visited Binn na Port at half past eight in the morning, the grass still wet with dew, the Sun burning off the last morning mists. As I climbed the slope between the two battlements, I was accompanied by a dozen red admiral butterflies, fluttering from grass tuft to grass tuft a few yards in front of me, pausing now and then to spread their showy black, white, and flame-orange wings, soaking up sunlight, drying out, adjusting their bodily thermostats. I paused too, in sync with the insects, letting sweat cool my body. The red admiral is big, colorful, kerchief-conspicuous. It migrates to all parts of Britain and Ireland from its winter home in central or southern Europe. All summer long it frolics in northern heaths and gardens, feeding and breeding. Then it flies south again. It is difficult to imagine how these mere slips of bright tissue, these origami insects, manage to flap their way from Spain to an Irish mountain slope. What impulse drives them north? What possible evolutionary advantage do they gain that would impel them on that long journey, impeded by broad sea crossings and summer gales? The red admiral's migrations are as deeply mysterious as the wanderings of people out of central Eurasia that brought to this mountain the builders of the fort.

Why a fort in this place? Steve MacDonogh of Dingle, who knows as much about the antiquities of the peninsula as anyone, believes Binn na Port had more to do with religion than defense, ceremonies of inauguration or assembly, and he may be right. Certainly, I have not seen within the protected part of the plateau any of those depressions in the turf that might indicate sites of ruined *clochauns* (circular stone dwellings), as can be found at Binn na Port's sister promontory fort Caherconree, at the other end of the Dingle Peninsula on a jutting shoulder of the Slieve Mish Mountains, or at many coastal promontory forts of an apparently defensive nature.

Although Binn na Port and Caherconree have many similarities, the latter structure is more impressive architecturally and commands a more strategic location at the landward end of the peninsula. Caherconree figures prominently in stories of Cu Roi, chieftain of the people known as the Érainn. He was a magical person, possibly divine, who carried off to this fortified promontory the beautiful Blathnaid, daughter of the king of the Isle of Man, upon whom the Ulster champion Cu Chulainn had also set his eye. Cu Chulainn pursued his beloved, guided by magical birds, and after a few misadventures along the way met Blathnaid near the fort. Together, they plotted Cu Roi's death. Returning to her unsuspecting partner, Blathnaid whined that the stones in the wall of the fort were too small, not nearly large enough to impress an enemy. Cu Roi sent his men out of the fort to get bigger stones. Blathnaid then poured milk into a stream that flowed down the mountain, a prearranged signal for Cu Chulainn that the defenders were away. The rest of the story works itself out in the usual way, with the set quota of combats, betrayals, and tragic ending. It is impossible to climb to Caherconree today without half expecting to see the stream beside the path run white with milk. That Binn na Port does not have a similar role to play in the ancient stories suggests that it was never called upon for use in dire events.

MacDonogh guesses that another function of the fort was display. When the walls stood tall and unbroken, they would have made an intimidating impression on anyone approaching by land or sea, he says, a symbol of confidence and power. But if visible symbolism was the motive for the considerable effort that must have gone into collecting these stones and piling them into massive ramparts, we would have to assume that the weather was fairer thousands of years ago than today. The odds that any potential attacker might see the fort from below under present conditions of almost continual cloud would have hardly made the construction worthwhile. Archaeologists date the fort from the late Bronze Age or early Iron Age, which means within the last few centuries before the Christian era and not long after the Celtic invasions. If so, typical weather then was probably not much different than today. Climatologists tell us on the basis of pollen studies that weather on the Atlantic fringe in Celtic times was far from balmy. About 500 B.C. a long stretch of warm, dry conditions gave way to falling summer temperatures and wet, cloudy oceanic weather (fewer pines, more birch). The impressive battlements of Binn na Port were probably therefore no more likely to have been seen from afar in the time of the Fianna than they are today.

But the date of the building of the fort is far from certain, and even the rather vague guesses of the archaeologists must be accepted with caution. The early history of Ireland is one of successive invasions of peoples coming from the south and west, out of the great heartland of Eurasia, a geographic pot always boiling over with people on the move. Irish myth identifies six successive waves of intruders, sometimes identified by a prominent warrior-hero: of Cessair and her mostly women followers; of Parthalon and his people, who all died of plague; of Nemed, also ill-fated; of the (so-called) small, dark, and boorish Firbolgs; of the clever and magical Tuatha De Danann, the fairy race; and finally of the "Milesians," or Gaels, with their iron spears. None of the rich texture of myth surrounding these supposed invaders is of much use to archaeologists, who identify successive migrations by their enduring artifacts. Thus we have the Stone Age pioneers entering Ireland as the glaciers retreated and the seas rose, with their crude stone tools and shell middens; the Boyne culture, named for the massive passage tombs at the bend of the Boyne River north of present-day Dublin; Late-Neolithic culture, with its "wedge-grave" single burials; the Beaker people; the Food Vessel people; the Urn people; the Bronze Age; the Iron Age; and so on.

A large part of what we know of these people is related to their deaths: tombs, grave goods, skeletal remains. Successive waves of invaders held the conviction that some part of the individual persists at least temporarily after death and maintains a relationship with the living community. Providing the dead with food, clothes, even furniture and companions, was thought necessary to maintain their continued existence. Commerce between the living and the dead was assumed as fact. (The belief in a ghostly community existing side by side with the living persisted in rural Ireland into modern times, although at variance with Christian dogma.) How the Indo-European invaders imagined life after death is not always clear. Middle Eastern sources from the same period represent it as "a rather weakened and gloomy form of the physical world . . . cold and especially dry," a far cry from the bright and fruitful paradise of Christianity and Islam. On the evidence of the Irish myths, death, even a peaceful death, is a kind of cutting down, a grim reaping, never "natural," never "accidental," always prefigured by signs and omens. Death for the Celts was a cusp between two worlds, partaking of each, confounding opposites. One might choose to die bravely in battle, or for love of a woman (or fairy person in mortal guise), but no one chose to die, as Mediterranean Christians sometimes did, expressly to achieve the other side.

What is certain is that ideas of life and death along the Atlantic fringe were special in their melding of many traditions. Elsewhere in Europe a people pressed by Asiatic expansions could move westward in waves of successive displacement, carrying local customs and racial characteristics unmodified into fresh territories. But on the Atlantic fringe there was nowhere to move in the face of a successful invasion except into the cultural and genetic blender. No wonder the idea of a Land of Delight in the Western Sea took hold on this strifeful shore. And no wonder that crossing that sea should become so fitfully tangled up with that other great crossing-over, which was death.

How many different cultural waves lapped up against the walls of Binn na Port is not clear, but I'm inclined to believe that this fortified mountain was primarily a place of refuge where people could retire under threat. Their lives were at stake, given the barbarity (by our standards) with which victors then treated the vanquished, but ideas were at stake too. Presumably the defenders felt their own fates were tied up with those of their gods, and so Binn na Port may also have been—as MacDonogh suggests—a place of religious significance, the very inaccessibility of which ensured proximity to the deities. The first generations of Christian holy men in Ireland, Brendan included, often took themselves to the mountaintops and seagirt isles to live and pray, and certainly a belief that severe, inaccessible places were in some sense sacred did not appear full-blown with these Christian hermits. Something of a hankering for communion with wild nature must already have been part of the pre-Christian Celtic spirit. Today, Christian pilgrims still make their way to the tops of Ireland's holy mountains, Brandon and Croagh Patrick, and to the grim, bare sea rock of Skellig Michael; what draws them there is an expression of their faith, of course, but they may also be acting out a script embedded in Irish culture since pagan times, a sense of correspondence between the wild and the holy.

THERE IS A TENDENCY IN our more technologically and scientifically advanced era to think of our European ancestors of two thousand years ago, especially those of the wild Atlantic fringe, as less intellectually advanced than ourselves. But these were a people, remember, who were contemporaries of Plato and Aristotle, Archimedes and Euclid, Ovid and Lucretius. Their brains were fully developed, their thoughts complex. The physical circumstances of their lives may have been hard, but the texture of their lives—loves, hopes, fears, dreams—was every bit as subtle as our own. We read of the hero-warrior Diarmaid, for example, who had a mole on his face that made him irresistible to women (including the young and beautiful Grainne, who forced Diarmaid to elope with her, though she was betrothed to the aging Fianna chieftain

Fionn Mac Cumhail, provoking a seven-year pursuit of the intemperate couple up and down the length and breadth of Ireland that finally led to Diarmaid's death and Grainne's marriage to Fionn), and we think of super-model Cindy Crawford's trademark mole. Loves, passion, clothes, music, cosmetics, decoration—pluck a few pre-Christian Celts from Binn na Port, drop them into present-day Dublin, and after a few moments' disorientation they would no doubt adapt to the rhythms of modern life. Even their dress might be considered marvelously chic.

I suspect that what might most surprise a pre-Christian Celt dropped into twenty-first-century Dublin would be the relative absence of violence. The Celtic myths are chock-full of epic battles and single combats between heroes (although as we see them portrayed in the ever-popular books on Celtic mythology, these conflicts are dressed up in bloodless garb). Life on the Atlantic fringe was never easy; death was always present. The grim sanctuary of Binn na Port suggests a people huddled in a cold, wet place, with a minimum of shelter, waiting for the onslaught of their enemies. Defeat meant slaughter or slavery. There are hints in the ancient stories of hostages being buried alive, and disinterred skeletons of decapitated bodies are not rare. Some archaeologists suggest that the skeletal evidence supports human sacrifice as part of druidic culture. In any case, a lot of blood was spilled in the course of everyday life.

There is much ado these days about "Celtic spirituality," and indeed some aspects of the Celtic reverence for nature strike an affirmative modern chord, but we shouldn't forget that nature can be cruel and unforgiving, and that a tendency toward male violence is probably a genetic part of our nature. The coming of Christianity to Ireland was apparently effected without much bloodshed, but Christ's injunction that we should love our neighbors as ourselves did not stop the newly converted Irish, or Christians anywhere, from killing their neighbors with abandon. What makes our species unique on the planet, however, is our capacity to culturally mitigate genetically predisposed behaviors. What made Christ's message so revolutionary was the Golden Rule: Do unto others as you would have them do unto you. It is a message that the Fianna would have found inscrutable.

Of course, it is impossible to get completely into the minds of a people who left so few written records—only a few memorial inscriptions on tombstones in ogham script. Certainly we have a great body of legends (the Book of Invasions, the Red Branch Cycle, the Fenian Cycle, the King Cycle) that describe the history of pre-Christian times (the story of Oisin and Niamh is an example; that of Diarmaid and Grainne another), but all of these were written down long after the recorded events purportedly took place, and the stories are filled with magical incidents that render even the simplest assertions of fact unreliable. The myths must be read impressionistically, but even then they may tell us more about the minds of the Christian scribes who first wrote the stories down than of the pagan heroes and heroines, champions, and villains who are the protagonists of the stories themselves. One thing the legends do tell us is that early Irish Christians had no desire to erase their pagan past, but made every effort to preserve and accommodate pre-Christian history within the new theological perspective. This willingness to accommodate, at which Saint Patrick was apparently adept, may explain why the conversion of Ireland took place with so little spilling of blood.

ONE EARLY IRISH POEM MAY give us a glimpse into the minds of the builders of Binn na Port, especially because it reinforces what the archaeologists tell us about the pagan Celts. Titled "Song of Amergin," and sometimes called "The Mystery," it is attributed to one of the "Milesian" princes who supposedly colonized Ireland several hundred years before the birth of Christ. Tradition has it that these are the first verses made in Ireland, although it is unlikely that any written version of the "Song of Amergin" predates the sixth or seventh century, and maybe even later:

> *I am the wind on the sea.*
> *I am the ocean wave.*
> *I am the sound of the billows.*
> *I am the seven-horned stag.*
> *I am the hawk on the cliff.*
> *I am the dewdrop in sunlight.*
> *I am the fairest of flowers.*
> *I am the raging boar.*
> *I am the salmon in the deep pool.*
> *I am the lake on the plain.*
> *I am the meaning of the poem.*
> *I am the point of the spear.*
> *I am the god that makes fire in the head.*
> *Who levels the mountain?*
> *Who speaks the age of the moon?*
> *Who has been where the sun sleeps?*
> *Who, if not I?*

What we have here is not so much a poem as a litany, an invocation, a prayer, supposedly recited when Amergin first placed his foot on Irish soil. Certainly, the words are evocative, beautiful, mysterious. One can almost imagine a druid priest on the misty peak of Binn na Port invoking these phrases as part of a ceremonial rite whose origins are lost in the mists of time. The druid is surrounded by men, women, and children dressed in skins and coarse cloth, adorned with clasps, neckbands, and bracelets of bronze or gold; the men hold spears tipped with points of iron or swords forged with the swirling designs that Christian monks would later adapt to illustrate liturgical books such as the famed *Book of Kells*. Ruffles of cloud curl off the lip of the northern cliffs. The air is cold and damp, although it is high summer—the festival of Lughnasa. As the priest chants, a procession enters through the double gates, having made its way up from the mountain's foot on Brandon Bay. The leaders of the procession bear a stone head that will be ceremonially buried in the mountain's boggy turf. Once again Lug has symbolically defeated Crom Dubh; once again the Sun will be made to yield its grudging bounty. From the eastern horizon a flash of green tints the clouds, then an all-encompassing rosy hue. The gathered throng watches the rising Sun. *"Who has been where the sun sleeps?"* chants the priest, speaking for Lug. *"Who, if not I?"*

All of this is pure conjecture, of course, but of one thing we can be reasonably certain, and Amergin's litany would seem to confirm it: The people who worshiped at Binn na Port found their god in nature, in sea wind and ocean wave, in stag, hawk, salmon, and boar, in dewdrop and blossom. The god who makes fire in the head also makes the coming and going of the light, the green shoots of plants, the lowing of newborn calves. The speartip, too, and valor in battle. The Celts were a polytheistic people, but their concept of divinity was so general and pervasive as to amount to a kind of pantheism. Their many-faced divinities drew their efficacy from a perceived life force with a male and female aspect, first and foremost represented by the interaction of Sun and Earth. He/she tracked daily across the sky and warmed the seed in the soil, but also took the form of thunder and lightning, hound, bull, stallion, salmon. He/she presided over the land of Tir na nOg, across the Western Sea, where all went after death and feasting never ceased. As this life force permeated every aspect of the natural world, so it became the warp of legend upon which is woven the weft of human history.

I AM THE GOD THAT makes fire in the head. What makes the human species different from all other creatures is the fire in the head, the never-ceasing wonderment behind the eyes, the questions that fill the mind in the darkest hours of the night, the longing, the uncertainty, the perception of mystery. It is all there in the repertoire of the Celtic storyteller: the magical births, the youthful exploits, the wooings, the elopements, the adventures wrapped with miracles, the voyages in search of the Land of Delight, the heroic deaths and transformations. All animals and plants have sex, but only humans embellish the procreative act with romantic tales. (What county in western Ireland does not have a mountain crag known locally as the Bed of Diarmaid and Grainne?) All animals kill; only humans kill their own kind for honor or glory, or willingly surrender their lives for faith. The fire in the head, always burning. Everywhere. In the sea, in the deep pool, on the plain, in the mountain fastness. Burning, burning.

In his book on pre-Christian Ireland, the Irish scholar Dáithí Ó hÓgáin writes: "The human mind, in its attempt to unravel a mystery, tries to concretize and dramatize its components, in other words to think metaphorically. It is this metaphoric mode of thinking which gives rise to the calcified imagery which we know as superstition, and we can be sure that the earliest inhabitants of Ireland were just as adept at developing and preserving such traditional beliefs and practices as has man in every other time and place." And so we look back upon the religious beliefs and rites of the pre-Christian Irish as "superstitious," neglecting to recognize that our own responses to mystery are equally metaphorical and therefore equally likely to fall into "calcified imagery." The eighteenth-century philosopher Voltaire wrote of superstition: "A Frenchman traveling in Italy finds almost everything superstitious, and is hardly wrong. The archbishop of Canterbury claims that the archbishop of Paris is superstitious; the Presbyterians levy the same reproach against his Grace of Canterbury, and are in their turn called superstitious by the Quakers, who are the most superstitious of men in the eyes of other Christians." It is not always easy to draw the boundaries between reason and superstition, observed Voltaire. One person's sensible dogma is another person's nonsense.

Superstition is about the best word we have for looking down our noses on those who believe something other than what we believe ourselves. The word comes from the Latin verb *superstare*, "to stand upon or over."

According to the *Oxford English Dictionary,* the noun form *superstitio* probably originally meant "standing over a thing in amazement or awe." One modern meaning of the word—"unreasoning awe or fear of something unknown"—is close to the Latin root. More commonly, we use the word to mean "any irrational, groundless practice or belief founded on fear or ignorance"—such as (we are inclined to say) the animism and polytheism of the pre-Christian Celts. The Romans, who gave us the word, knew exactly what they meant by it: A superstition was anything strange and foreign to the Romans. The Roman writer Plutarch suggested that superstitious people did not use their intelligence when thinking about the gods, which led to fanaticism, and fanatics made bad citizens of the empire. For Romans, Christianity was the superstition par excellence, especially as Christians started to become more numerous within the empire. Successive Roman writers vigorously condemned the superstitious beliefs of the upstart Christians. Of course, when Constantine led the empire to Christianity in the fourth century A.D., suddenly superstition was on the other foot.

After Constantine, the Greek and Roman gods—Dionysus, Athena, Jupiter, Mars, and the rest of the Olympian pantheon—became the new superstition, and it was as superstition that we learned the Greco-Roman myths in school. We also learned of the "superstitions" of Hindus, Muslims, Native Americans, and all other peoples who professed something other than our own calcified metaphors. The strange rites of the druids, in oak groves or near woodland pools, of course, were superstitions of the most obvious sort. The idea that someone might bury the stone head of a god in a high place to influence solar cycles might have evoked from us a condescending smile, even as we Catholic Christians embraced beliefs no less arbitrary. Even in Roman times, the physician Galen warned his students and colleagues how easy it is to believe merely because we inherit the religious or philosophical beliefs of our parents, teachers, or native city.

We have a great capacity to deceive ourselves. Back in the 1940s, the behaviorist psychologist B. F. Skinner did a famous experiment with pigeons that he thought had some relevance to human superstitions. He put birds in the kind of cages used for training animals by reinforcement—peck a bar, get some birdseed, that sort of thing. Except in this new experiment, the feed was provided at regular intervals regardless of what the pigeons did. The pigeons fell into certain behaviors all by themselves—nodding, or turning, or pecking for food—although their behaviors had nothing to do with the reward being offered. Skinner wrote: "A few accidental connections between a ritual and favorable consequences suffice to set up and maintain the behavior in spite of many unreinforced instances." He added: "The experiment might be said to demonstrate a sort of superstition. The bird behaves as if there were a causal relation between its behavior and the presentation of food, although such a relation is lacking. There are many analogies to human behavior." Many analogies, indeed. Thus does metaphorical thinking become calcified.

How do scientists avoid falling into the trap of superstition? By relying upon double-blind experiments, placebos, reproducibility, peer review, unrelenting skepticism, and all the rest of the tricks of the trade we call the scientific method. Is scientific knowledge therefore immune to calcification? Of course not. Even as we hold our scientific theories to the refining fire of experience, we should remember the archbishops of Canterbury and Paris, and know that humans, like pigeons, may be genetically wired for self-deception.

Still, it is absurd to say, as many moderns do, that religion is *mere* superstition. Religion is the natural human response to the inexplicable in nature, the fire in the head evoked by mystery; to extinguish the response is to extinguish the fire. But what sort of response is appropriate in our scientific times? What response is consistent with a modern sense of our common humanity? How can awe, reverence, and the perception of mystery coexist with skepticism and empiricism? How can we think metaphorically, as we must, without becoming prisoners of our metaphors? I stand on Binn na Port, the Peak of the Fort, within stone walls millennia old, and feel the mystery all around me, the fire burning on this wild, cloud-shrouded shoulder of the mountain. There is a tendency, certainly cultural, perhaps genetic, to fall to my knees, to speak praise, to give thanks—but in what words, and to whom? The "Song of Amergin" comes easily to my lips, especially in this place, but they are not my words and do not reflect my world. My world is not the world of the salmon and the stag, but of the laptop computer and the telescope. What I share with Amergin is a sense that the world is shot through with mystery in ways that even our sophisticated science cannot begin to comprehend. In the face of that mystery I feel compelled to speak, *to pray*, but cannot find words that feel comfortable on my tongue.

I have an Irish-speaking friend who offers a different interpretation of the place name Binn na Port: not Peak of the Fort, as the name is commonly rendered, but Peak of the Music, from an alternate interpretation of *port*, "tune." And indeed the wind here does play a kind of unceasing music upon the instrument of rock and cliff, which is part of the wild charm of this high place. Saint Columbanus, a contemporary of Brendan, is supposed to have said, "If you wish to know the Creator, understand the creature." It is a thought that is perfectly consistent with pre-Christian Celtic spirituality, with the accommodating first generations of Irish Christians, and perhaps with our own scientific understanding of the world—if we too can effect an accommodation. But before we see how the accommodation might work, we must leave the fortress/sanctuary/aeolian instrument of Binn na Port and venture into the glacial corrie—every journey to enlightenment must pass through the dark valley—and experience for a moment the thrusting up of the mountains, the shift of continents, the leveling of high places, and the comings and goings of ice.

COUMAKNOCK
MOUNTAIN GLOOM,
MOUNTAIN GLORY

Unless you are more goat-footed than I am, and more fearless, there is no way off Binn na Port except back the way you came, through the gated double walls and down again to the pilgrim path. However, one need not descend all the way to where we left the path on the ridge above Faha; rather, one can angle down toward the place where the track reaches the lip of Coumaknock (mountain hollow), the largest of the glacial corries on Brandon's flank. A more adventurous way to ascend Brandon bypasses the lower part of the Faha pilgrim path altogether and follows (against the current) the Owenmore River as it tumbles down the mountain from its source at the corrie's headwall. There is no established track to follow on this latter route; one moves up along the rock-bound shores of a series of "paternoster" lakes strung out like the beads of a rosary, each lake becoming progressively smaller (and colder!) as you approach the valley's headwall. The ascent is like climbing a flight of stairs, a lake on each tread, a waterfall at each riser. The hollows in which the lakes are confined were carved by ice at a time when Earth's climate was cooler than presently and glaciers formed on the shadowed northern slopes of the mountain. Each basin represents a stage of the glacier's advance down the mountain or its subsequent retreat.

In the mid–nineteenth century, John Ball, an Alpine mountaineer, visited the steep-sided, bowl-shaped valleys on Mount Brandon's flank and noticed the similarity to valleys in Switzerland where living glaciers reside today. "Where you see the same effect, assume the same cause," wrote Isaac Newton, and Ball applied Newton's dictum here. If Brandon's valleys resemble in every particular (other than the absence of ice) the glacial valleys of Switzerland, then Brandon's valleys too were carved by glaciers, he asserted, and soon geologists agreed with him. Once people knew what to look for, evidence of the former ice was everywhere to be seen: in scoured and scratched bedrock; in massive boulders carried far from their source; in drumlins, eskers, moraines, and other morphological features manifestly associated with living glaciers, found in places—Ireland, England, New England—where no glaciers exist today. The idea of ice ages, when parts of the northern continents were covered by glaciers half a mile thick, was no less fabulous in its first tellings than stories of Cu Roi and Fionn Mac Cumhail. But—*if you know what to look for*—a walk into Coumaknock will convince even the most incredulous doubter; the valley walls are smoothed and scratched precisely as they are in places, such as the Alps, where glaciers reside today. So fresh are these evidences of ice in the upper part of Coumaknock that "one might imagine the Glacial Period was only just passed away," wrote the early-twentieth-century Irish naturalist Robert Lloyd Praeger.

Our scramble down from Binn na Port rejoins the pilgrim path on a more or less level track clinging to the valley wall high above the Owenmore River. Many times I have walked this path when the valley was filled with mist and only the sound of water falling from lake to lake confirmed the nearby chasm. At other times the mist cleared to reveal medallions of black water in the valley below and a pyramidal peak towering on the left, apparently the highest elevation around and easily mistaken by the first-time climber for our destination; in fact, the true summit of the mountain lies farther ahead. Inevitably, our level track must intersect the steadily rising valley floor, and this it finally does as we near the headwall. No exit from the valley appears possible. Steep and apparently unscalable cliffs rise on every side. But egress is possible, barely; a careful scrutiny of the headwall reveals a track sidling upward along the base of a sheer rock face.

Before we commence the vertical climb, we'll linger for a while in the valley, shadowed from any ray of the Sun, munch a candy bar, perhaps take a dip in the icy water of one of the many pools. In the few patches of soil along the path large-flowered butterworts (not nearly so large as their name implies) lift their sticky blue carnivorous blossoms to catch whatever insects come their way, and so survive on flesh where soil nutrients are rare. Ravens sail on updrafts; their croaking calls resound. Every sound reverberates from the corrie walls. Water seeps from the cliff face, gathering into drizzles, trickles, rivulets, streams; the valley walls are sheets of glistening wet. Nowhere on Mount Brandon is the skeletal structure of the mountain more vividly displayed than in these bare, damp corrie rocks; the ice-carved gash of Coumaknock is like a surgeon's incision that lays bare the mountain's sedimentary strata. For the modern mountaineer, these looping and twisted layers of rock are the corrie's most striking feature and confirm dramatically, if confirmation were needed, the stories told by geologists of ancient seas and shifting continents. Crossbedding can be observed at several places along the path: truncated strata intersecting at odd angles, the effect of wind on loose sand at a time when the material of these rocks was being deposited in a desertlike basin of the Old Red Sandstone Continent. It is no mystery how that long-vanished continent got its name; the rocks we walk across are red, rose, pink, salmon, maroon.

What did the Irish monks who walked here in Brendan's time make of the exposed strata? Doubtless they would have avoided this bleak hollow except when seeking refuge or a place of exceptional solitude. But *then* what did they think? Did they puzzle over the folds of rock, the tumbled boulders, the scratches, the crossbedding, and wonder at their cause? Almost certainly not. They most likely assumed that every feature of the mountain was as it had always been, fashioned by the Creator during the seven days of creation, as described in Genesis, and in this they set themselves apart from their immediate ancestors.

Curiously, among all the legends that have come down to us from the pre-Christian Irish there are no creation stories—no equivalent of Genesis or the other creation stories of the eastern Mediterranean. It is hard to think of any other people in the world who do not have among their lore an account of how the world began. Irish history does not start with a first man and woman, fashioned by a deity, but with an invasion of a land already occupied and already old. Of the making of the Sun, Moon, and stars, of the raising of the mountains, of the origin of animals and plants, we have nothing. Only now and then in the Irish myths do we hear of events that explain in some fabulous way a particular feature of the landscape, such as the huge boulders that hang on the walls of the glacial valley near Anascaul, east of Dingle. Here, according to legend, Cu Chulainn did battle with a giant who attempted to carry off the woman Scal ni Mhurnain (another abduction!). Cu Chulainn and his opponent took up positions on the cliffs at opposite sides of Anascaul Lake and taunted each other in verse (how wonderfully Irish), and then, when their verses fell flat, hurled boulders at each other across the valley for a week. The boulders still litter the valley. This taunting and rock flinging are as close as we get in Irish myth to an explanation for a landscape. Heroic deeds, to be sure, larger than life, but not a divine creation; just two outsized protagonists hurling rocks. Irish folk stories from the pre-Christian period (as written down, admittedly, by later Christian scribes) never record interventions of a deity who exists independently of nature. Only when continental Christianity imposed its predominantly transcendent theology on indigenous Celtic Christianity in Ireland, at about the time of the Viking incursions, did miracles *that interrupt the course of nature* become part of the fabric of Irish life.

THE EARLIEST NATURAL HISTORY OF Ireland is that of Gerald of Wales, who visited the island in 1183 and described what he observed in a book dedicated to the English monarch Henry II. For Gerald, as for all other Christian writers of his time, the question of origins had been answered once and for all by the divinely inspired book of Genesis. Whatever was to be seen in Ireland had been there since the beginning. He mentions, for example, the "Brendanican mountains" of the west and tells us that the soil of Ireland is "soft and watery" (how true in Kerry). Even at the tops of mountains you will find pools and swamps, he says. He lists the animals of Ireland and describes their natures. All of this is accurate enough and sounds surprisingly modern. But most of Gerald's pages are taken up with the bizarre and the exceptional: a wolf that talks with a priest; a goat that has intercourse with a woman; a woman with a beard and a mane on her back; seed cursed by the bishop of Cork that does not grow. For Gerald, the exceptional occurrence was of more interest than the general course of events. God did not just set the world going at the beginning then step aside; his interventions in the world continued on a daily basis.

Gerald's preoccupation with miracles contrasts sharply with the writings of Saint Patrick, which are less concerned with the exceptional. Irish Christians of Patrick's time apparently saw no need for an outside deity to meddle in the creation; their God was thoroughly at one with the creation, animating every instance of the here and now. Whatever happened, even unusual events, happened according to what we would now call natural law. Since, in this Celtic view of things, all of nature was in some sense divine, there was no need for the miraculous. This opinion, by the way, is not uniquely Celtic; Saint Augustine of Hippo said something to the effect that the one great miracle is existence itself. Origen, a third-century Alexandrian and father of the Church, also flirted with this idea (things that are done by God may appear to be unbelievable, he stated, but they are not contrary to nature); it is perhaps not without significance that Origen hailed from the city of the protoscientists Eratosthenes and Aristarchus.

We know that the pre-Christian Celts and their predecessors in Ireland were close observers of the natural world. Their detailed knowledge of the motions of Sun, Moon, and stars is evidenced by their many astronomically aligned tombs, stone circles, and ranks of standing stones. Their festivals, as we have seen, were linked to the solar motions. The first generations of Irish Christian priests seem to have inherited from their druidic predecessors a keen interest in the workings of nature, and their learning is surprisingly eclectic. "Irish Christianity was a faith in which the material world was welcome," writes the scholar Marina Smyth. There was nothing in Patrick's version of Christianity that precluded an interest in natural law. On the contrary, Christianity gave the Irish saints and scholars an intellectual link to the Continent that reached all the way to the homelands of Aristotle, Eratosthenes, and Archimedes. Bits and pieces of eastern Mediterranean science were taught in Ireland at a time when most of Christian Europe was languishing in mysticism and magic.

Science is not a modern invention. It did not begin with Galileo and Newton. Natural philosophers of the eastern Mediterranean, residing mainly at Alexandria during the centuries immediately preceding the Christian era, invented every element of what we now understand to be the scientific way of thinking: organized skepticism, the primacy of reason, the interplay of theory and observation, mathematics, quantitative empiricism, the exclusion of the miraculous. Early triumphs of the method dazzle us even today, such as Aristarchus's determination of the sizes and distances from the Earth of the Sun and Moon, or Eudoxus's theory of planetary motion. But all of this came to a screeching halt with the rise of Christianity and its emphasis on otherworldly reality. The scientific way of knowing would not again make substantial progress until Renaissance secularity knocked orthodox Christianity from its pedestal.

Geology did not develop as a science as rapidly as astronomy, and the reasons are clear. For one thing, the time scale of geologic change is vastly longer than a human life, or even human history, whereas the heavenly bodies perform their regular permutations on a daily and yearly basis. Aristotle and Pliny the Elder, among other Greek and Roman natural philosophers, made stabs at explaining geologic phenomena in terms that were not miraculous. For example, the waters that seep from mountain walls, gathering into rushing streams, posed the kind of puzzle that intrigued Aristotle. How did it happen that the water inside a mountain was never exhausted? Rain falling from the heavens must have something to do with it, he reasoned, but also might not air condense into water as readily inside the Earth as it does above it? "For mountains and high ground, suspended over the country like a saturated sponge, make the water ooze out and trickle together in minute quantities but in many places," he wrote. Aristotle wrestled, too, with the meaning of fossils and was convinced of their relation to living organisms, though how the fossils came to be in the rocks was unclear. In any case, he believed in a great age for the Earth, which made it possible for him to imagine that sea and land might exchange places by processes too slow to observe historically. And so, even in

ancient times, the elements were in place to provide a natural explanation for the twisted strata of Coumaknock.

However, once Christianity ordained the Genesis
seven-day creation as literal truth—metaphor calcified—
scientific geology was stopped in its tracks. With only a
few thousand years to play with (the Earth was created on
October 23, 4004 B.C., declared the seventeenth-century
bishop James Ussher), any naturalistic explanation of fossils, for example, was put in abeyance. Instead, the
divinely contrived flood of Noah was evoked to explain
shells on mountaintops. The ammonite fossils that are
common in sedimentary strata near Whitby, England,
were attributed to the miraculous intervention of Saint
Hilda, seventh-century founder and abbess of the convent
at Whitby, an early convert to Christianity. According to a
widely accepted medieval account, Hilda turned snakes
to stone, a miracle that one-upped Patrick, who merely
drove them out of Ireland; the creatures in the rocks were
serpents, the biblical manifestations of Satan, petrified by
Hilda's saintly powers. I doubt very much if Hilda, or
Patrick, or any thinking person of her time and place,
would have entertained such an explanation. Hilda was a
scholar, a patron of poets, a teacher, and a wise counselor.
Her spirit was in the background of the Synod of Whitby,
at which leaders of the English Church adopted Roman
liturgical practice (which, ironically, may have presaged
the end of the nonmiraculous thinking of Hilda and her
pagan forebears). Of course, we have no way of knowing for sure what Hilda thought of fossils, or if she considered them at all, but one species of fossil ammonite,
Hildoceras, has been named by modern geologists for the
holy scholar-abbess of Whitby, an honor that in the long

history of human learning will stand her in better stead than a whole province full of "petrified snakes."

JOHN CAREY, A LECTURER IN the Department of Early and Medieval Irish at the National University of Ireland, Cork, has provided us with translations of many texts from the time of Patrick and later. We learn three things from the texts, he says. First, the early Irish Christians sought, "with agile and audacious imagination," to make room for the old religion within the confines of the new; second, they were open to broader European culture, including classical science; and third, they were aware of the unique and hybrid nature of their heritage. Fed by "a restless and visionary curiosity," they forged a vigorous amalgam of art, literature, learning, and spirituality, which they then carried to the European mainland by founding dozens of monastic establishments. This was the generation of Irish "saints and scholars," characterized by a harsh eremitic discipline and, almost incongruously, a passion for beauty and learning.

For several centuries, polytheistic paganism and monotheistic Christianity lived side by side in Ireland, influencing each other, giving rise to a predominantly immanent Christian theology that contrasts sharply with the predominantly transcendent theology of the Continent. This uniquely Irish brand of Christianity survives into modern times, says Carey, as "a rich and equivocal mixture of magic and devotion, of prayers, charms, legends, fairs, and pilgrimages, which wove together Christian teaching and the surviving vestiges of paganism." But quite aside from the enduring magical elements of Irish religious practice (which are now

vanishing even in the countryside), it is the quasi-pan-
theistic character of early Irish Christianity that most
concerns us here. Saint Columbanus was not the only
Christian of his time to emphasize the creation as the
primary revelation, but in Irish Christianity the idea
took hold and resisted for some time the notion that the
only reliable revelation is to be found in Scripture or
tradition mediated through the Church of Rome. This
latter view was destined to exert an unfortunate sway
within Christianity—a sure prescription for a faith that
is static, triumphalistic, bureaucratic, and idolatrous.
Not for nothing did Constantine, with his eye on the
consolidation of empire, opt for a transcendent, im-
mutable, and unitary God whose relationship with the
world was codified once and for all in the politically
efficacious doctrines of Nicaea.

Granted, continental orthodoxy never entirely abandoned the notion that God might reveal himself through
the creation, but the emphasis has been on *through* rather
than *in*. In the common formulation, God is *author* of the
book of nature, not to be confused with the book itself.
The historical tension between transcendence and
immanence (at work in *every* religious tradition) was
decided in continental Christianity in favor of transcendence. By contrast, the early Irish texts suggest a God
who is more fundamentally immanent in every part of
the creation—in Sun, Moon, stars, wind, and wave—
even as the unutterable mystery of the universe confounds our understanding and perception. Saint
Columbanus asked in a sermon: "Who shall examine the
secret depths of God? Who shall dare to treat of the eternal source of the universe? Who shall boast of knowing

the infinite God, who fills all and surrounds all, who enters into all and passes beyond all, who occupies all and escapes all?" Those who wish to know God, he says, "must first review the natural world." In the early Irish Christian understanding, exceptional events occur not because of the interventions of a supernatural deity who temporarily suspends the ordinary course of things, but rather because of the divine potentialities inherent within nature itself. For the authors of the early Irish texts, a reluctance to believe in "the full extravagant strangeness of existence" was tantamount to blasphemy, says Carey. The early Irish monks were certainly awake to the ineffable mystery that permeates every moment of existence, but they were also interested in whatever ancient scientific writings they could find. They applied their learning even to the explication of the so-called miracles of Scripture, seeking "natural" explanations for the wondrous stories of the Bible.

Here was a defining question for Christianity, and indeed for Western civilization: Is the action of the Creator (however we might understand the agency by which the universe came to be and is sustained) manifested in miraculous intrusions of the transcendent—a wolf that talks with a priest, seed that is cursed by a bishop and does not grow—or in the extraordinary quality of ordinary events—the rising and setting of the Sun, the call of the cuckoo, the rainbow, the aurora, the dew on the grass? We know how the issue was officially decided by the early councils of the Church to the detriment of ancient science, but in Celtic Christianity we catch a glimpse of what might have been. Here is a verse from *The Psalter of the Quatrains,* a series of poems of the ninth or tenth century that covers the full sweep of Christian sacred history and draws upon sources as diverse as Pliny the Elder, Augustine, and the Old Testament. The verses (translated by John Carey) are full of astronomy, numerology, and natural history, but the prevailing spirit is one of reverence for the Creator as manifest in the creation.

> *My King of mysteries, of fair fame,*
> *wherever in his creation he dwells above the world,*
> *mighty and glorious—in my life*
> *I can do nothing but worship him.*

It is not hard to imagine Brendan traversing Coumaknock, ascending or descending from his hermitage on the summit, exulting in the grandeur of the folded walls, the trickling streams, the flat black sheets of water unrippled by any wind, and making a prayer to the King of mysteries. But once theologians of the continent had wrested the Creator *out* of the creation (thereby placing access to him in the hands of the priests and the institutional church), the mountains became fearful places, devoid of the divine and partaking of the fallen nature of matter itself. Thus they acquired the "mountain gloom" described by Marjorie Hope Nicolson in her study of mountains in European literature.

When Adam and Eve were cast out of the garden, they were in a sense cast out of nature itself, out of the wonder-filled world of the pagan polytheists. "Cursed is the ground for thy sake," pronounced a peeved deity in Genesis, and this is the theology of corrupted nature that John Milton describes in *Paradise Lost*. When Eve bit into the apple, "*Earth felt the wound, and Nature from her seat, / Sighing through all her works, gave signs of woe."* As Nicolson makes clear, for European writers of the Middle Ages, and right down to the new beginnings of geologic science in the eighteenth century, mountains were savage places, unredeemed, to be avoided. Dante's description of climbing the Mount of Purgatorio could easily be a description of the headwall of Mount Brandon's Coumaknock:

> *Up through the riven rock we made our way;*
> *Cliffs hemmed us in on either side; the ground*
> *Beneath called feet and hands both into play . . .*
> *Surpassing sight, the summits pierce the sky . . .*
> *Forcing myself, I crawled up after him*
> *Until the ledge was underfoot at last . . .*

But whereas a climber of Dante's time might make the ascent with fear and trembling, the modern mountaineer, or even Sunday trekker, achieves that final ledge with a sense of exhilaration and, whether the ridge is calm or blowing a gale, knows that the moment is one to be savored. Between ourselves and Dante stands a renaissance of Alexandrian science, called the Scientific Revolution, in which all of nature was, as it were, redeemed by reason, lifted out of its fallen state as defined by Christian dogma, and restored to a morally indifferent continuity of calm and gale, Sun and rain, valley and peak, light and dark, summer and winter, health and sickness, full belly and famine, all of it riddled with mystery and surpassing our understanding, but inspiring in both our knowledge and our ignorance a sense of awe.

Carey says of the early Irish texts: "Understanding

the world's mysteries can move the soul to worship, and so can failure to understand them. In finding a road to God in their experience of nature, the Irish celebrated a universe which is not sundered from its Maker." The sundering he speaks of had already occurred in the gnostic mystery cults of the Middle East, which flourished alongside Alexandrian empiricism, and which infected Mediterranean Christianity from the beginning. Irish Christianity was initially spared the blight of gnostic spiritualism by its cagey accommodation of druidic pantheism. But pantheism is not an effective religion to buttress an empire, because it assumes that God is to be found everywhere, whereas an empire must have a strong center (what was later to be called "the divine right of kings"). Constantine understood this when he took the Roman Empire to Christianity and, at Nicaea, codified a theology that was compatible with the consolidation of power at a single seat. Christ's divinity was an issue at Nicaea, and it served Constantine's purpose to make Christ divine. The Incarnation was, in the post-Nicaean dispensation, a one-off intrusion of the divine into nature, terminated when Christ rose from the dead and ascended into heaven. Any further participation of the Creator in the creation (as, for example, in the transubstantiation of the Eucharist and miraculous cures attributed to saints) would be administered by the hierarchical authority of a centralized Church.

The Protestant Reformation of the sixteenth century shattered the hegemony of the Roman Church. The Scientific Revolution of the seventeenth century reasserted that nature is not a fallen mess making "signs of woe" but an amoral *given* to be studied and, if possible, understood—thereby pushing back ever so modestly the bounds of our ignorance. The "new" science of Galileo and Newton makes possible recovery of the idea that all things are shot through with divinity, which seems to have been the attitude of the earliest Irish Christians. Expressions of celebration and awe do not require a ticket stamped by a bishop.

One early Irish document especially attracts our attention: *On the Miracles of Holy Scripture* by Augustinus Hibernicus, the "Irish Augustine," an Irish monk writing in the year 655, probably in a monastery at Lismore in County Waterford. The author asserts a belief that the so-called miracles of Scriptures must be interpreted within a context of nature's laws, not in contravention of them. As Carey says, the book has elements that might strike the modern reader as fantastic, even comical, but "particularly impressive, and so far as I know unparalleled in the early Christian West, is [the author's] vision of nature as a harmonious whole whose integrity not even God will violate." This uncompromisingly naturalistic view of the world might have been considered heretical by the standard of orthodox continental Christianity, but it is perfectly compatible with post-Galilean science.

EVERY LANDSCAPE HAS BOTH A real and an allegorical quality. Thus we speak of Ireland as the Land of Saints and Scholars, imbuing its lush green fields of today with an aura of its medieval past. In these pages, too, Mount Brandon plays two roles: geographic and metaphorical. The pre-Christian Celts of Ireland populated the landscape with fairy folk, who lived in groves and wells, in palaces under the hills, and on isles in the Western Sea. Their religion amounted to a kind of animism, with every feature of the landscape possessed of a living spirit. In his book on religion in pre-Christian Ireland, Dáithí Ó hÓgáin writes: "The human imagination, at its most primitive level, reflects its own feeling or personality onto other phenomena with which it has to contend. In this way, the environment could be felt to be comprised of a great variety of very definite agencies, and man's encounters with these agencies were naturally to be explained in human terms." Much of this prehistoric animism survived into Christian times, and traces can be found in the Irish countryside even today. Christian monotheism had a moderating effect on druidic animism—and drove the fairies from their hills—but by and large the Christian God is still imagined as a humanlike agency (in spite of the cautioning advice of Columbanus and others), and we speak of *him* as a *person,* consider prayer a *conversation,* and call him *Father*, *Lord,* and *King.*

He who would wish to know God "must first review the natural world," said Columbanus, wisely, but we must be careful that we don't look into the world as into a mirror, seeing only animistic projections of our personhood. The mathematical way of knowing invented by the Alexandrians and revived by Galileo and his successors provides us a way to examine the world without (or minimizing) encrustations of human allegory. And so it was that in the early 1800s British and Irish cartographers sought to make a map of the Irish landscape in a way that reproduced in every particular the actual physical landscape and made no reference to its allegorical or metaphorical significance. Thousands of years earlier, Eratosthenes of Alexandria had laid down the principles of scientific cartography, including a system of longitude and latitude, and in the second century A.D. Claudius Ptolemy of Alexandria produced an atlas of the known world that would be the standard of physical exactitude for more than a millennium. But this early start to mathematical mapmaking had been aborted by a brand of Christianity that focused attention on allegorical landscapes—heaven, purgatory, hell—the imaginary territories of Dante's *Divine Comedy*.

In 1824 the British Parliament authorized the mapping of Ireland on a scale of six inches to one mile, to arrive at a more equitable system of land taxation. No countrywide survey had ever before been attempted at this scale, not even in Britain itself. The first step in this gigantic project would be a primary trigometric survey that would define precisely the general form of the island. Forty-five hilltop locations scattered about Ireland were selected to be the vertices of a spiderweb of triangles. If the three interior angles of a triangle are known, the relative sizes of the sides of the triangle can be exactly computed. If many triangles share sides, as was the case within the spiderweb, all that remains is for one side of one triangle in the web to be precisely measured and the whole web is determined. To this end, a baseline was laid out along the shore of Lough Foyle in County Derry and measured with unprecedented precision. From there a net of interlocking triangles was cast over Ireland. The long residence on wild mountain summits required for the survey made the work both dangerous and difficult.

Sometime in 1840 the surveyors reached the summit of Brandon, lugging to the top their massive theodolite, a telescopic instrument for measuring angles. Waiting for clear days, they peered through their instrument to other stations on hilltops across Dingle Bay, at Taur Mountain to the east on the Cork-Kerry border, and even as far away as Bencorr in Connemara. On exceptionally clear days, I have sometimes caught a glimpse of the Aran Islands from Brandon's summit, sixty-five miles away, but seeing a glint of reflected sunlight (from an instrument called a heliostat) or, at night, the gleam of a limelight lantern from a Connemara mountaintop thirty miles farther on strikes me as a nearly miraculous act of patience, given the Irish weather. The maps that resulted from this Herculean project are objects of great beauty and remain today the defining representation of the island upon which the Irish project their human affairs. When we bought our piece of property in Kerry, a map based on the original triangulation of Ireland was used to denote the transaction, the field boundaries having remained essentially unchanged for more than a century.

The cartographers of the Ordnance Survey were followed by the geologists, who added to the maps colors representing the rocks of Ireland, and notations for faults, strike, dip, and other indicators of the disposition of the strata. In the dark corries on Brandon's flanks they teased out stories of valley-filling glaciers and the crumpling of sedimentary strata over eons. By the time of the survey, the Enlightenment had taken firm hold in Europe and mountain gloom had given way to mountain glory. The twisted rocks on the valley walls vastly predate the supposed sin of Adam and Eve in 4004 B.C.; like the Celtic myths, the geologic story of the rocks recedes into a time without a beginning. We now understand that the Earth has been laboring for billions of years to bring forth these hills, and the forces of erosion have labored just as long to cut them down. From what we can tell, none of this modern story would have disquieted the faith of Augustinus Hibernicus or Columbanus. The rocks and the glacial scratches on the rocks reveal a creative agency that infuses every grain of silica or crystal of ice. No Middle Eastern creation myth with tree and serpent speaks half so eloquently of the Mystery of Mysteries as the ice-scoured walls of Coumaknock.

"If you wish to know the Creator, understand the creature," said Columbanus. It would be a mistake, of course, to look too closely at a particular time and place in history for instructive antecedents to the present. The Irish saints and scholars lived in a narrow wedge of earth and sky on the edge of the known world; we live in a universe of a hundred billion galaxies (at least). When Carey suggests that Augustinus Hibernicus's world of lawful harmony was an early foreshadowing of our modern "ecological sensitivity," he is careful to add "tentative and isolated." Still, there is something about the worldview of the people who lived on the Atlantic fringe two millennia ago that meshes pretty well with the worldview of the modern geologists who tell us a new story of the mountains. "In seventh-century Ireland, there clearly was a consciousness of nature and of its intrinsic value which felt no need to refer back to Christianity for its justification," writes Marina Smyth. The most attractive thing we find in the early Irish Christian texts is an intense curiosity about the natural world—*this* world—and a sense that everything in it is holy.

SUMMIT
DISCOVERY OF IGNORANCE

Summit of Mount Brandon

S<small>PREAD OUT ON A TABLE</small> by my desk is the Dingle
Bay sheet of the Geological Survey of Ireland, a lovely,
large-scale multicolored map showing all the rocks of
the Dingle Peninsula and much of the Iveragh Peninsula
across Dingle Bay. Most of the rocks date from the
Upper Paleozoic era of Earth history (the map informs
me), between 300 and 400 million years ago, the era of
"early life," when the first amphibious creatures were
moving out of the seas onto the land, insects took wing,
and parts of the continents were covered with vast
swampy forests. Continents were on the move then, as
always, riding the great mobile sheets of Earth's crust
called plates. An ocean called the Iapetus was being
squeezed out of existence as continents collided to form
the Old Red Sandstone Continent, so named by geologists for the beds of red sandstone rock that were laid
down at that time. The part of Earth's crust that is now
the wave-swept Dingle Peninsula was then somewhere
in the interior of that continent. There are no marine
fossils in the Dingle formations, only the fossilized bur-
rows of terrestrial worms, so we know the basin in
which these rocks were deposited was dry. Crossbedding
in the rocks also suggests windblown sedimentation.
Toward the end of the Paleozoic, about 250 million years

ago, a second mountain-building thrust, associated with the approaching collision of Africa and Europe to the south, crumpled the sandstone strata and forced them skyward.

I trace on the geologic map the track of my ascent, from Faha to the summit, through Coumaknock. There are no dramatic geologic variations. The map shows one color for the length of the path, a pale olive. It is labeled BM, and the accompanying booklet identifies the rock as "Ballymore Sandstone Formation," rhythmically bedded layer after layer of firmly consolidated sediments, more than a half mile thick. In the ice-carved walls of Coumaknock the folds of these strata are beautifully revealed. As I ascend the headwall, up through the strata, I am making a journey through millions of years of time, during an epoch about 400 million years ago when these rocks were deposited. (Imagine how long it took to deposit sediments more than a kilometer thick!) The 1,500 years that separate us from Saint Brendan are as nothing compared to the abyss of time by which we are distant from the burrowing creatures that lived on the Old Red Sandstone Continent.

Aristotle, Leonardo da Vinci, Nicolaus Steno, and others had caught glimpses of the eons during which mountains were thrust up and abraded with imperceptible slowness, but not until the Scotsman James Hutton articulated a notion of geologic time in 1785—wresting time from the theologians who insisted upon Bishop Ussher's chronology and a literal interpretation of Genesis—did the deep history of the Earth became apparent to all but the most recalcitrant scriptural literalists. With millions, perhaps billions, of years to play with, new explanations for the mountains became possible. Geologists of the nineteenth century ranged the hills and valleys, looking at the rocks with fresh vision, and a new story began to reveal itself, a story in which the planet was not merely a stage for human history but had a long—almost unimaginably long—history of its own. In the booklet that accompanies the Dingle Bay sheet of the Geological Survey of Ireland is a bibliography listing all of the relevant published works that contribute to our present understanding of the peninsula's geology. The earliest of these works is a paper of Richard Griffith from 1845, followed shortly by papers of Joseph Beete Jukes and George Victor Du Noyer from the 1850s and 1860s. These men tramped the Dingle Peninsula (indeed, all of Ireland), mapping the rocks, looking for patterns, teasing out explanations in conformity with the principles laid down by Hutton, of subsidence, sedimentation, uplift, and erosion, taking place over eons of time. They were followed by dozens more geologists, right down into our own time—the bibliography lists them all—each adding another detail to the story. One of the most recent papers (1995) is titled "The Discovery of a New Devonian Tetrapod Trackway in SW Ireland," an account of fossil footprints, evidence of one of the planet's earliest amphibians walking on dry land.

The discovery of geologic time stands as one of the greatest intellectual divides that separate us from our ancestors. What happened with the publication of Hutton's book was not simply a stretching out of historical chronology, from six thousand years to billions of years; the real breakthrough was the discovery that the creation of the universe can (and must) be understood in terms that make *no reference* to the human drama. From

1785 onward, the mountains are not merely backdrop scenery—gloomy or glorious—for human history; rather, human history becomes part of a grander story that includes the rise and fall of mountains. It was an epochal transformation, and we are still learning how to deal with it. The ancient anthropomorphic gods we created in our likeness retain their grip on our imaginations. We have grown used to our presumed cosmic centrality, and we are reluctant to surrender our self-appointed primacy as lords of creation.

Curiously, our struggle to adapt to a universe whose age is measured in billions of years is aided by insights of the early Irish Christian writers, precisely because they were heirs to—and to some extent assimilated—a Celtic worldview that (insofar as we know) made no reference to a temporal creation. The pre-Christian Celts looked back not to a moment of time within historical memory when the world and all who are in it were created ex nihilo, out of nothing, but to successive waves of ancestors, receding into the unremembered mists of time, who arrived on Ireland's green shores from the east and south. The modern view of human origins is remarkably similar. Humanity had its start, paleontologists and geneticists now tell us, in East Africa, several million years ago, and migrated from there to the four corners of the Earth. The Atlantic shore of Ireland was one of those corners—about as far as you can get from the evolutionary Eden.

THE CLIMB OUT OF COUMAKNOCK achieves the ridge a few hundred feet below the summit of Brandon. You never know what to expect when you reach the top of the headwall. Almost certainly there will be wind off the Atlantic. As often as not, mist. If you are lucky, when your head rises above the lip of the precipice a vista opens out as grand as any you are likely to see in Ireland: the end of the Dingle Peninsula in all of its rugged grandeur, with its red sandstone ridges extending out to sea as a string of islands reaching westward. On a clear day, you might almost believe that if you stood on tiptoes you could see Newfoundland or Cape Cod out there on the far horizon. Often I've wondered if Brendan might have stood here, staring out to sea, mesmerized as to what lay beyond the black pyramid of Tearaght, the farthestmost island, inhabited then, as now, only by seabirds.

Rain or shine, calm or gale, a short tramp up a well-trodden path now brings you to the summit. The summit of Mount Brandon is a half dome; to the east, cliffs fall vertically into Coumaknock; to the west, a long boggy slope descends to the village of Ballybrack. Most climbers prefer to ascend the mountain by the Faha track, with its dark cliffs, wild waters, and steep headwall, rather than the gentler path from Ballybrack. Their reason might be summarized in lines penned by the young Alfred Lord Tennyson, caught up in the mountain glory that had, with the Age of Enlightenment, cast gloom aside:

> *All hail, Sublimity! thou lofty one,*
> *For thou dost walk upon the blast, and gird*
> *Thy majesty with terrors, and thy throne*
> *Is on the whirlwind, and thy voice is heard*
> *In thunders and in shakings; thy delight*
> *Is in the secret wood, the blasted heath,*

The ruin'd fortress, and the dizzy height,
    The grave, the ghastly charnel-house of death,
In vaults, in cloisters, and in gloomy piles,
Long corridors and towers and solitary aisles!

From what we know of the early Irish saints, lingering in the influence of Celtic pantheism, these lines of Tennyson might have struck a chord with them. Did Brendan walk Brandon's craggy paths with similar emotions? Is not Tennyson's paean to sublimity near in tone to this verse from the *Altus Prosator* (Exalted Creator), a hymn of twenty-three verses sometimes attributed to Brendan's sainted contemporary Colum Cille?

By the divine powers of the great God
the globe of the earth is suspended, and the circle of the
    great abyss set,
held up by God, by the mighty hand of the Omnipotent.
Columns support it like bars,
promontories and cliffs, firm foundations,
like pillars planted and immovable.

Whoever wrote the *Altus Prosator* (here translated by John Carey), the verses are filled with thunder and lightning, darkness and grim beasts, fertile delights and the shining stars of Orion—in short, the full panoply of worldly wonders, glorious and terrible, which speak to awestruck worship of whatever godly power animates the world.

THE SUMMIT OF MOUNT BRANDON today is the locus for a curious mix of artifacts. The first thing one sees as one approaches the apex is a large hardwood cross, which recently replaced a somewhat flimsier cross made from the spars of a German aircraft that crashed in the "Airplane Valley" during World War II. At the base of the cross are the ruins of a rectangular structure called Saint Brendan's Oratory, supposedly the place where Brendan kept his solitude before setting out on his Atlantic voyage. There is a cross-inscribed stone of medieval origin; a cairn of stones piled high by pilgrims in ages past; foundations of a square stone structure that might have been a sheltering place used by pilgrims; extraordinarily, for such a height, a "holy well," a rectangular depression in the soil filled with water, now rather unappetizingly covered with algal slime, but, with proper maintenance, easily able to quench a pilgrim's thirst; and, finally, the sort of concrete pillar that one finds on almost every summit in Ireland, put in place by the Ordnance Survey of Ireland, beginning in 1959, for the purpose of triangulation (now made redundant, of course, by a new kind of electronic triangulation using satellites).

One summer day several years ago, I sat shivering in fog with a friend on the summit of Brandon when a man in shorts and sneakers came jogging up out of the mist. We chatted, and he told us his story. He was seventy years old. Much against the advice of his family, he had sailed alone to Ireland from England's Isle of Wight and his small boat was anchored in Brandon Bay near the foot of the mountain. That morning he had rowed to shore and pedaled his collapsible bike to Faha, then jogged up the mountain. Pleasantries exchanged, he bid us goodbye and trotted back off into the mist. My friend and I sat there munching our soggy sandwiches, not knowing whether to be exhilarated or depressed: exhilarated to know that we might still be achieving the summit a decade hence when we turned seventy; depressed to know that even now the Englishman would leave us panting in his wake. According to some accounts, Saint Brendan was in his sixties when he made his retreat on the mountain-top and then set sail for the Land of Delight. Presumably, his response to the mountain was not all that different from that of our English visitor or of ourselves. If we correctly interpret the early Irish Christian writings, all of nature was then considered gloriously holy, anointed with the grandeur of Amergin's pantheism, not yet dragged into gloom by the sin of Adam that would, in the post-Nicaean Church, infect everything earthly with the taint of perdition. Now, again, in our own time, the mountain has been returned to glory, as Marjorie Hope Nicholson tells us, by the Enlightenment and the invention of geologic science—Eden reclaimed. *I am the wind on the sea, I am the ocean wave*, we sing with Amergin. *I am the mountain that rises in the mist.*

Geologic time—cosmic time—was certainly the greatest intellectual discovery of the post-Enlightenment century. It may be more accurate to speak of a *rediscovery* of cosmic time; the Greeks entertained a notion that the world might be eternal, and, as we have seen, the pre-Christian Irish seem to have felt no need to account for a beginning. But it was one thing to see human history receding into mists of unknown duration, and another to have before your eyes visible evidence of the eons of time proposed by the nineteenth-century geologists. If I were to pick a moment in history when the idea of cosmic time became indelibly anchored in Western thought, it would be a fine day in 1788 when James Hutton took his friends

James Hall and John Playfair for a boat ride along the Berwickshire coast in Scotland. He took them to a place along the cliffs where he had deduced beforehand they might find strata of Old Red Sandstone lying almost horizontally across truncated vertical strata of even more ancient sedimentary rocks. (A similar disposition of strata can be seen in the cliffs at Sauce Creek on the northern flank of Brandon.) Hutton outlined for his friends the long episodes of uplift and erosion, occurring in cycle after cycle, that were required to create this particular arrangement of layered rocks. Grain by grain, sand was deposited and turned to stone; millimeter by millimeter the sandstone strata were lifted, tilted, and squeezed to create the vertical strata; grain by grain these strata were truncated by erosion; millimeter by millimeter the truncated surface subsided; grain by grain new sand was deposited and subsequently turned to stone; millimeter by millimeter these rocks were raised and eroded, presenting at last the configuration that Hutton displayed to his friends. How long these events took, Hutton was not prepared to say: certainly, millions of years, perhaps tens of millions. John Playfair recorded his impressions of that day on the Berwickshire coast: "On us who saw these phenomena for the first time, the impression will not easily be forgotten. . . . The mind seemed to grow giddy by looking so far into the abyss of time."

Geologic time, time that extends into the past without apparent limit, rescued the Old Testament from the false presumption of literality. The concept of geologic time made possible modern geology, biology, physics, and astronomy, none of which could have developed within the straitjacket of the six thousand years allotted to the creation by the literal exegetes of Genesis. It removed from nature the stigma of Adam's sin. For those who understood and accepted the implications of geologic time, nature became again, as for the contemporaries and near contemporaries of Saint Brendan, Columbanus in particular, *the primary revelation of the Creator.* The nineteenth-century geologists who tramped these mountains unraveling the riddles of the rocks not only gave nature a history that was independent of human history, but also glimpsed a creative power—a divinity, if you will—that is more, much more, than an exalted version of ourselves. This last consequence deserves further reflection, but first there is another modern discovery that must be noted, of equal or greater importance than the discovery of geologic time: the discovery of ignorance. And this too, it turns out, the early Irish Christians anticipated.

THE PHYSICIAN-ESSAYIST LEWIS THOMAS wrote: "The greatest of all the accomplishments of twentieth-century science has been the discovery of human ignorance." The science writer Timothy Ferris agrees: "Our ignorance, of course, has always been with us, and always will be. What is new is our awareness of it, our awakening to its fathomless dimensions, and it is *this*, more than anything else, that marks our coming of age as a species." It is an odd, unsettling thought that the culmination of the scientific quest—the long slow gathering of reliable knowledge—should be the confirmation of how *little* we understand about the universe we live in. *Our coming of age as a species,* Ferris calls it. How did such a revelation come about?

The discovery of ignorance followed inevitably from

the discovery of geologic time. John Playfair grew giddy looking into the abyss of time; he had no idea of its depths, only that vastly more years were required for the deposition and erosion of the rocks than those allotted to human history. Today we ascribe an age to the universe of 12–15 billion years. With our telescopes we observe at least 100 billion galaxies—perhaps there are an infinite number—each, typically, with tens or hundreds of billions of stars, each star possibly with planets. In such a universe we are clearly permitted to know only a smattering of what might be. A few bold physicists have suggested that it might be possible to discover the ultimate laws of nature—what physicist Stephen Hawking has called "knowing the mind of God"—but even this is likely to be a futile quest. Galaxies as numerous as snowflakes in a storm! Each possibly with uncountable planets, strange geographies, biologies, intelligences. To live in such a universe is to admit that the human mind singly or collectively will never be in possession of final knowledge. "The more we learn about the world, and the deeper our learning," wrote the philosopher Karl Popper, "the more conscious, specific, and articulate will be our knowledge of what we do not know, our knowledge of our ignorance. For this, indeed, is the main source of our ignorance—the fact that our knowledge can be only finite, while our ignorance must necessarily be infinite."

How do we react to this new and humbling awareness of what we do not know? That depends, I suppose, upon our personal temperaments. Some of us are frightened by the vast spaces of our ignorance. Others are exhilarated by the opportunities for further discovery, for the new vistas that open before us, and revel in the

frisson of fear and excitement that accompanies the myr-
iad new worlds that swim into our ken. It is this latter
frame of mind that drives the scientific quest. The physicist Heinz Pagels wrote: "The capacity to tolerate complexity and welcome contradiction, not the need for
simplicity and certainty, is the attribute of an explorer.
Centuries ago, when some people suspended their search
for absolute truth and began instead to ask how things
worked, modern science was born. Curiously, it was by
abandoning the search for absolute truth that science
began to make progress, opening the material universe
to human exploration."

The discovery of our ignorance should not be con-
strued as a negative thing. Rather, ignorance is a vessel
waiting to be filled, permission for growth, a ground for
the electrifying encounter with mystery. In the early years
of the twenty-first century, we can claim with enthusiasm
that we know both more and less than we knew at the
beginning of the twentieth century: more because our
inventory of reliable knowledge has been greatly
expanded, less because the scope of our ignorance has been
more fully realized. "No thinking man or woman ought
really to want to know everything," notes Timothy Ferris,
for when "knowledge and its analysis is complete, thinking stops."

NOT FAR FROM MY KERRY cottage, in a farmer's field
marked by the degraded remnant of a ring fort, a hole in
the ground gives entrance to a meandering network of
underground chambers, eleven chambers in all, cut from
subsoil and bedrock and shored up here and there with
stones. When my kids were young, they explored this

dank warren with flashlights, crawling through tiny passages deep under the hill while I fretted nervously outside. No way I would enter that subterranean maze! There are places near the tunnel's entrance through which I could barely squeeze. Archaeologists call this mysterious structure a *souterrain* (under earth). There are hundreds of them on the Dingle Peninsula, and many more throughout Ireland, Scotland, Cornwall, and Brittany. No one is certain of their purpose. Souterrains are often associated with places of habitation—ring forts, commonly—and may have been built as temporary refuges in times of danger. Perhaps they were used for storage of foodstuffs or valuables. It has even been suggested that they might have provided cosy sleeping accommodations during inclement weather. None of these theories strikes me as convincing, although I can think of no more likely alternative. Nor is it certain when the souterrains were built. The incorporation of stones inscribed with ogham script or crosses into the sides and roofs of some tunnels indicates a construction date in early Christian times, possibly after the sixth century A.D., but to me the underground chambers have the look of something from an earlier era. Surely these structures were known throughout medieval times and must have been equally mysterious then. I wonder if they might have given rise to the tales of fairy palaces under the hills.

It is easy to dismiss the fairies and their subterranean domiciles as products of overactive and uncritical imaginations, but surely the fairy folk of western Ireland are no more far-fetched than the miracle lore I was asked to embrace as a child, or indeed certain theories of science that I tentatively hold to be true today. Scientific knowledge of the universe does not differ from fairy lore by being less fantastic, but in the nature of the evidence that is adduced to confirm it and the purpose to which it is put. I sit on the summit of Mount Brandon and look out across the end of the Dingle Peninsula. Cottages dot the landscape, more and more holiday homes each year. Those bobbing specks of color in the fringing sea are lobster boats, pulling pots. Two prominent lines—rocky ridges—point toward North America, rising above and dipping below the waves. One ridge includes the cliffs of Ballydavid Head, the peaks of the Three Sisters across Smerwick Harbor, Sybil Head, and the islands Inishtooskert and Tearaght. The other ridge includes Mount Eagle, Dunmore Head, the Great Blasket Islands, and the islands Inishnabro and Inishvickillane. These ridges no doubt continue under the sea out there beyond the farthest island; they are the much eroded sign of a crumpling of the rocks that took place 300 million years ago. At that time the place where I sit was at the heart of a much higher mountain range in the middle of the Old Red Sandstone Continent, far from any ocean. Beneath the insulating rock of the continent, heat accumulated in the hot, almost molten interior of the Earth. The white-hot rock beneath the rigid crust began to circulate in great convective loops, tugging the crust this way and that. Huge slabs of crustal rock slipped along faults, lifted and fell. About 200 million years ago, the continent was decisively torn down the middle, and east and west began to move apart. Where the crust separated, molten rock oozed up from below to fill the cracks, creating new crust, dense ocean-floor rock that did not rise as high as the less dense continents. Water from other parts of the planet's surface flowed into these new basins. The Atlantic Ocean was born!

North America began its journey away from Europe. That was 200 million years ago; today the continents are two thousand miles apart. All that time the Atlantic has been widening at a rate of about an inch a year. Each summer, I must travel an inch farther on my journey from New England to Dingle. Meanwhile the mountains have been wearing down; Brandon surrendered the greater part of its bulk to the floor of the sea, and the flanking ridges, pointing to North America, gradually have been slipping beneath the waves. It is an astonishing story, no less fantastic than stories of fairy palaces under the hills, and I cannot get it out of my mind as I sit on Brandon's summit looking westward. The story is confirmed by geologic evidence of many sorts: fossils, rock types and ages, seafloor sediments, and so on. An unmanned submarine has descended to the mid-Atlantic rift and photographed sizzling lava oozing into cracks, new seafloor for a widening sea. But the cinching evidence for a widening ocean would be to directly measure the distance from Dingle to Boston, say, with an accuracy of inches, and show that the ocean is getting wider. Remarkably, this can now be done by a method known as Satellite Laser Ranging, which involves bouncing a laser beam off a satellite equipped with a reflector; the time required for the light to make a round trip pinpoints a site's location with extreme accuracy. Another method is borrowed from astronomers and is known as Very Long Baseline Interferometry. Two widely separated dish antennae—in Europe and the United States, say—record radio signals from a distant source, typically a galaxy (or quasar) billions of light-years away. The slight differences in the arrival times of the signals are recorded with atomic clocks. The time differences, which are due to the finite velocity of the radio waves and the minute differences of distance from the source, are as small as a few thousands of a second. If these differences are measured for at least three different sources, it is possible to precisely calculate the distance between the two receivers. For antennae in Massachusetts and Sweden the distance does indeed increase each year at the rate predicted by geologists.

I love the idea that radio waves from distant galaxies—energy that has been traveling across space for billions of years—can be harnessed to confirm that North America and Europe have been moving apart for hundreds of millions of years. When I was in school fifty years ago, we knew nothing of drifting continents. We knew nothing of quasars or lasers or Very Long Baseline Interferometry. Within my lifetime, whole continents of knowledge have been explored. The landscape of our learning has expanded prodigiously. And so have the territories of our ignorance.

RECALL FOR A MOMENT THE early Irish Christian writer Augustinus Hibernicus, the "Irish Augustine," author of *On the Miracles of Holy Scriptures*, a book that attempts to show that all of God's works in the world must act in accordance with nature, not in opposition to it. The following passage in Augustinus is worth quoting in its entirety.

Let whoever desires true wisdom make haste to the eternal kingdom where there is no ignorance; meanwhile, let him say in the words of the teacher of the gentiles, "We know in part, and we prophesy in part." For we barely understand even in part all of the things which we possess. The surface of the earth on which we toil, by which we are nourished, kept alive and supported, appears plainly before our eyes; yet even so we do not know what holds it up. The sun is assigned to minister to us by day, but the course which it follows in the night is hidden from our knowledge. Who has the wit to understand the changes of the moon, waxing in fifteen days and waning in the same interval? We are allowed to behold the surges of the flowing sea, but are denied knowledge of the place to which it ebbs. We know and are mindful of the day of our own birth; but the day of our death, although it is certain that it will come, is unknown to us. We are only able to perceive in part even the bodily things which we can see. Thus we know only in part, for as long as we are in this world.

It is an extraordinary passage, because what it says has been so rarely affirmed—by theologians or by scientists—and almost never before our own time. Throughout most of the Christian era, truth has been sought in Holy Scriptures—presumed to be divinely inspired—and these, being finite, can, in principle at least, be entirely known. Thus evolved a false sense of conviction, *an arrogance of certainty*. From such assurance were derived the burning of heretics, holy wars, pogroms, religious imperialism, and all the other wretched excesses that have betrayed the Sermon on the Mount. But if, as Saint Columbanus confidently asserted, the primary revelation of the Creator is *the creation*, it is inevitable that we shall see only through a glass darkly and prophesy only in part. He wrote: "If then a man wishes to know the deepest ocean of divine understanding, let him first if he is able scan that visible sea, and the less he finds himself to understand of those creatures which lurk below the waves, the more let him realize that he can know less of the depths of the Creator."

The phenomena of nature spread before us—Earth, Sun, Moon, sea, and tides—are steeped in mystery, as Augustinus Hibernicus and Columbanus remind us. Of course, we understand today much of what was a mystery to them: why the Moon waxes and wanes, for example, and where the water goes on the tide's ebb. We have traveled beneath the waves in submarines and photographed what lurks there. But for every puzzle of nature that has been unraveled, greater mysteries have become apparent. What is the origin of the Moon? What is gravity, and how does it relate to the other forces of nature? Why are the laws of nature one thing rather than another? Why is there a universe at all?

THE FLORA AT THE SUMMIT of Mount Brandon is sparse. Not much grows in the thin, infertile soil, out of which most nutrients have been leeched by rain. But blossoms of pink thrift soften the otherwise hardpan top of the mountain, sinking their taproots deep in search of whatever nourishment they can find. "I am the fairest of flowers," wrote Amergin, traditionally the earliest of Irish poets; he knew that the miracle of growth partook of divinity. I know more than did Amergin about how flowers grow. I know, for instance, how a "four-letter" chemical code along the dancing spiral of the DNA ensures that the blossom will be that of thrift and not of heather. So I add to

Amergin's revelation: *I am the fairest of flowers. I am the dance of the DNA. I am the language of amino acids. I am a blossom assembled from atoms of carbon, oxygen, hydrogen, and nitrogen according to a chemical script shared in part by every living thing on Earth.* Knowledge is an island in an infinite sea of mystery; as the island grows, so does the shoreline along which we encounter the mysterious.

The conversion of Ireland to Christianity occurred, almost uniquely in the history of proselytism, without notable martyrdom or violence. For several centuries Christian and druidic priests lived side by side, in what seems—given the intolerance of later Christian centuries—remarkable pacifism. This mutual forbearance is perhaps not so puzzling in a culture that affirmed, by both Christians and druids, the Mystery that soaks every speck of creation. From what we can tell, the earliest Irish Christians were more intent on celebrating the creation than on asserting abstract dogma. As John Carey says of Augustinus, and by extension others of his time and place: "A sense of the sacrosanct integrity of nature is one thing which we can draw from [his writing]; another, surely, is a vision of the miraculous at work all around us."

7

ATLANTIC
THE NEW STORY

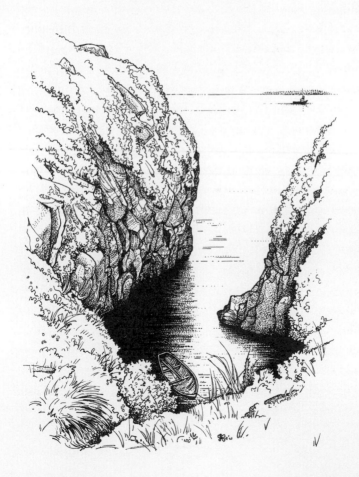

Nowhere in Ireland is one far from the sea, and in the west, especially, the sea encroaches deeply upon the land in bays and estuaries. Contemporaries of Patrick and Brendan went to sea in boats made of animal hides, and not always willingly. It seems to have been a common punishment of that time to set a convicted lawbreaker adrift in a tiny craft of one skin only, without oar or paddle, sometimes shackled, as far out to sea as a white shield might just be visible from the land. No food or drink was provided, nor indeed much in the way of clothing. Sometimes a favorable wind might blow the malefactor directly back onto the shore; more often he or she (and the punishment was often meted out to women) drifted away, never to be heard from again. The idea was to leave the ultimate fate of the criminal in the hands of God. One story tells of Patrick inflicting this fate upon a person known as Mac Cuill, who was apparently a rather unlikable brute: "His thoughts were evil, his words haughty, his deeds wicked, his temper angry, his body given to sin, his mind cruel, his life pagan, his conscience vain." One would think that such a fellow would not merit mercy, but apparently God had other ideas. Mac Cuill was blown to the Isle of Man, where he subsequently lived a saintly life, dying a bishop. It is somewhat poignant to think of all those unfortunate men and women of the early Christian centuries drifting hither and yon in tiny boats, like messages in bottles, sometimes washing up on distant shores.

The Dingle Peninsula is the westernmost land of Europe, so it is perhaps not surprising that strange things occasionally appear on its coasts. The region's Lusitanian flora and fauna apparently arrived by sea. The earliest recorded instance of *human* maritime visitors was an invasion by the so-called king of France, in the late pre-Christian period of Irish history. The story (which would not have been written down until very much later, and then in multiple versions) begins, as so many Irish stories do, with the abduction of a beautiful woman, in this case a double abduction. It seems that Fionn Mac Cumhail, leader of the Fianna, was visiting France. Smitten by the king's wife and daughter—and they presumably enamored by him—he carried the two women off to Ireland, much to the Gaulish king's chagrin and ire. The king gathered his allies, including twenty other royals and their armies, and sailed for Ireland. Eventually, the fleet arrived in Ventry Harbor, near the end of the Dingle Peninsula, where its many boats crowded the bay. As the continental warriors disembarked, they were met on the beach by Fionn Mac Cumhail, with the Fianna and their allies. The battle that ensued lasted a year and a day and left at the end not a warrior standing. Whether this story has a foundation in fact no one can say, but don't tell that to my neighbors in Ventry, who like to regale tourists with accounts of the epic clash of arms. They will point out local place names—Cluain na Fola (Field of Blood) and Cúin na dtréan Fhir (Slaughter of Mighty Men)—that prove (they say) the authenticity of the tale.

Rather more reliable are accounts of the day in the spring of 1927 when Charles Lindbergh's *Spirit of St. Louis* drifted in off the misty Atlantic, banked through Mám na Gaoithe (the Windy Gap), and buzzed the sleepy parish. The plane flew off to the south across Dingle Bay, toward Valentia Island, then on to Paris, successfully completing the first solo air crossing of the Atlantic. Valentia Island is where the first Atlantic telegraph cable came ashore in 1858, and where a trans-Atlantic telegraph station remained until 1966.

Between the respective arrivals of the king of France and Lucky Lindy, the Dingle Peninsula had other notable visitors from the sea. In 1580 a force of about six hundred Italians and Spaniards arrived in Smerwick Harbor, just over the hill from Ventry, to help Irish Catholics throw off the Protestant English yoke. The invaders ensconced themselves with their Irish allies in an Iron Age promontory fort at the edge of the harbor, Dún an Óir (the Fort of Gold), built up the eroded ramparts, and awaited the inevitable response by the soldiers of Elizabeth I. It was not long coming. An English army under the command of Lord Grey of Wilton—including, it is said, the infamous Walter Raleigh—soon had the rebels pleading for mercy. None was granted. Almost the entire garrison was put to the sword or hanged. Many heads were lopped from bodies, and Good Queen Bess was greatly pleased. Today, decapitated Catholic heads (in stone, of course) look down from a monument memorializing the massacre.

Not far away is Blasket Sound, where ships of the Spanish Armada took refuge from a storm on their circuitous (and humiliating) way home from defeat at the hands of Francis Drake and his plucky fleet of English sailors. On October 1, 1588, the armed galleon *Santa Maria de la Rosa*, battered by wind and wave, went to its watery grave with all lives lost but one. The victims may have included Prince D'Ascoli, the bastard son of King Philip of Spain.

Later, there were anticipated incursions from the sea that did not materialize. On almost every high prominence around the seaward rim of the peninsula are watchtowers, built either in Napoleonic times by the English to watch for a backdoor invasion of the British Isles by the French, or in the 1940s by the neutral Irish to keep an eye out for planes and ships of both the Axis and the Allies. The Irish have had reason enough to keep their attention fixed on the sea.

Other visitors from the Atlantic are noted only by naturalists. Tropical fish and sea animals from the Caribbean sometimes find themselves swept by currents north and east, and end up on Irish coasts. Now and then on Ventry Beach we have spectacular invasions of jellyfish, rounded up cowboy-style by circulating currents in Irish coastal waters and flung onto our sand by a southwest wind. Jellyfish go with the flow, and in the west of Ireland the flow is usually out of the sea, bringing to these shores ships of the Armada, tropical fish, and wind-assisted flights from North America by birds, butterflies, and Lucky Lindy. Going the other way, westward, requires rather more effort and no small amount of ingenuity.

FROM THE SUMMIT OF BRANDON on a clear day one looks down to the northwest on Brandon Creek, a gash in the Old Red Sandstone cliffs that buttress the northern flank of the mountain. Here a stream from the mountain has carved a passage to the sea, and the sea has widened the passage into a narrow high-walled gap, like a castle gate, in dark conglomerate rock that opens onto a tiny harbor. A one-lane road winds down the cliff to a slipway at the bottom, where several Dingle curraghs, the traditional fishing boats of the peninsula—made of wood laths and tarred canvas—rest upside down on their timber stands like shiny black beetles. A modern fishing boat or two might be anchored in the harbor, although in a northern gale this L-shaped nick in the rockbound coast would not offer much protection.

On May 17, 1976, Saint Brendan's feast day plus one, Tim Severin and four crew members set out from this harbor in a boat of lath and oxhides in an attempt to repeat the saint's purported sixth-century voyage to America. Severin's craft, the *Brendan*, was modeled on the traditional Dingle curragh and made entirely of medieval materials: leather, oak, ash, and flax, but unlike the present-day craft, which are powered by oars only, the *Brendan* carried sail. Brandon Creek is the traditional place where the saint began his journey. Severin is a man who has made a career of repeating mythical or semihistorical journeys of discovery: the voyages of Sinbad the Sailor, Jason and the Argonauts, and Ulysses, among others. His purpose with the *Brendan* was to show that the *Navigatio Sancti Brendani, Abbatis* (the Voyage of Saint Brendan, Abbot), the tenth-century manuscript account of a voyage supposedly made four centuries earlier across the northern Atlantic, might not be as far-fetched as many people have supposed. After many adventures, some of which were similar to purported experiences of the saint,

Severin and his fragile craft achieved the coast of New-foundland. His published account of the crossing, *The Brendan Voyage,* became an international best seller.

My wife and I learned in Catholic school that Saint Brendan discovered America; Leif Eriksson and Christopher Columbus were Johnny-come-latelies, according to our Irish teachers. But there is nothing in the *Navigatio* to reliably confirm an Atlantic crossing; nor is it certain that there is a historical basis to the tale at all. Stories of voyages upon the Western Sea are common in Irish mythology, including the story of that other adventurer, Bran, who (according to local lore) took his departure and made his return at Brandon Head on the other side of Mount Brandon. It is easy to imagine that the Christian saint Brendan and the mythical pagan voyager Bran might have become confused in the minds of later scribes. Nevertheless, Tim Severin was impressed by the many elements of the *Navigatio* that paralleled his own adventure—an iceberg, for example, might easily be the model for the floating crystal island encountered by Brendan—and he believes that the Brendan story has a historical basis. The fact that Severin's craft made it (barely, and with occasional assists by modern technology) to North America proves nothing, of course, except that such a voyage is possible. The modern adventure was an epic achievement regardless of the historicity of the *Navigatio,* and a fitting homage to the early Christian monks who lived in the shadow of Ireland's second highest mountain.

WE KNOW WITH CERTAINTY THAT the monks made sea voyages, probably in boats not much different from the one that Severin sailed to North America. In these craft they participated in an intellectual commerce back and forth across the Irish Sea and across the arm of the Atlantic that separates Ireland from the European continent. Some ideas that came westward to Ireland had their origin as far away as Egypt; what went eastward was an amalgam of Christianity and Celtic pantheism that made scant headway against a theology that emphasized the transcendence of God rather than his immanence.

In his book on Celtic spirituality, *Where Three Streams Meet*, Father Seán Ó Duinn says of the fairy faith (*creideamh sí*) of pre-Christian Ireland: "While Christianity has during its history shown a marked tendency to become involved in abstruse theological discussions and dogmatic formulations, the *creideamh sí* was primarily concerned with putting bread and butter on the table, with the secrets of nature and herbs to provide health and well-being, with good law to produce a stable society." He may be idealizing a society that cultured its own share of violence, but something of the fairy faith endured in the Irish countryside into recent times and was always anchored in the fields, homes, and holy wells rather than the churches. Devotions with paganistic elements can, of course, be found in the peasant faith of every European country, but in Ireland they seem to have found a more congenial *theological* reception, at least at the beginning.

What Celtic Christianity offered Europe was a religion of celebration and praise, in which God is manifest in every element of everyday life. What official othodoxy on the Continent (and ultimately in Ireland) embraced instead was a religion of abstruse theology that underscored the fallen state of nature and promised a redemption that could only come through the agency of the institutional Church. The God I found on offer as a child was to be found not in the fields and springs but in churches, and the pious Christian had to pay the price of admission.

The brand of transcendent Christianity that held Europe in its grip for more than a thousand years put a brake on science. Among the Alexandrians of the second and third centuries B.C., especially, geography, astronomy, and medicine were brought to a high state of development, knowledge of enormous practical use. But most of this scientific lore was lost when Europe turned away from nature and focused its attention upon a spiritual otherworld. It was no longer the mystery of the *everyday* that excited the curiosity of intellectuals, but the *exceptional* event, the presumed miracle. Even when I was growing up as a Roman Catholic child in the 1940s and 1950s, it was the miraculous which I was given to understand gave meaning to life, not the extraordinariness of the ordinary. The most dramatic difference between the tenth-century *Navigatio* and Tim Severin's account of his own twentieth-century voyage is the predominance of the fabulous and miraculous in the former and the fastidious celebration of the ordinary in the latter. Yet I have the feeling that if Brendan, the fifth-century Irishman, sat down with Severin, they would have more in common than would Severin and the miracle-obsessed tenth-century scribes who gave us the written accounts of Brendan's voyage.

Another Irish Catholic priest who is involved in the revival of Celtic spirituality, John Ó Ríordáin, calls his little book *The Music of What Happens*. He takes his title from an Irish story of the hero Fionn Mac Cumhail. Fionn asks his followers, "What is the finest music in the world?" They suggest answers: the cuckoo calling from the hedge, the ring of a spear on a shield, the baying of a pack of hounds, the laughter of a gleeful girl. "All good music," agrees Fionn. "But what is best?" they ask. Fionn answers: "The music of what happens." Like Seán Ó Duinn, Ó Ríordáin is attempting to recapture something of the mix of Celtic immanence and Christian transcendence that was forged by the Irish of the fifth and sixth centuries, a religion of the Gospels that does not look down its nose upon pagan wisdom.

As Christianity took hold in northern Europe, a pervading question was what to do with the old gods, the deities of the druids, the fairy faiths. Two strategies were employed, according to John Carey: euhemerism and demonization. In the first, the gods of the pagans were held to be humans who lived long ago, and who came to be worshiped after their deaths because of some extraordinary quality of their lives; in other words, the gods were not divine at all, but confabulated mortals. In the second case, the gods of the pagans were held to be demons: supernatural beings, yes, but wholly negative in character. Neither device was employed in Ireland between the time of Patrick and the coming of the Vikings, the so-called Age of Saints and Scholars.

The Irish, by contrast with the Continent, held the old gods to be supernatural but not evil. To this end, they imagined them as half-fallen angels, spiritual beings who did not join the rebellion of Lucifer, but who were nevertheless expelled from paradise to Earth, where they live in close harmony with nature. Another approach on the part of the Irish was to imagine the pagan gods as descendants of Adam who somehow escaped the corruption of the Fall. Either way, these immortal fairy folk were thought to exist in a state of grace, free from Original Sin. Both Irish strategies for saving the old gods were unorthodox, indeed heretical by continental standards, and were of course eventually submerged in conventional theology, but the fairy folk survived into modern times pretty much as the early Irish Christians imagined them.

All of this may seem embarrassingly artificial: a matter of the early Irish Christians trying to have their pagan cake and eat it too. By any modern standard of scientific thinking, it all seems rather silly. But we are not required to judge an earlier age by modern standards. The essential point here is that for early Irish Christians, all of nature was enchanted—*the music of what happens.*

None of this could have happened anywhere except on the edge of the world, on the wild fringe of Christendom, which was wild only in its removal from Rome (first in its secular, then, after Constantine, in its religious authority) and its proximity to the apparently limitless sea. It seems to me that the Western Sea has not yet been fully appreciated as a source of the uniquely Celtic brand of religious thought. Many times I have sat on the summit of Brandon looking out at the Atlantic, stretching away in its apparently limitless extent. The sight of the sea takes a firm hold on the mind, a kind of dulling rapture. It becomes almost hypnotic. Recall that the Irish, in all of their respective waves of identity, reached their land by crossing narrow bodies of water. The English Channel is but a short step. The Irish Sea is also a modest barrier; on a clear day you can see Ireland from Scotland. But at the end of the Dingle Peninsula the land seems to dribble

off into infinity, a teaser of increasingly small islands—
the Great Blasket, Inishnabro, Tearaght—pointing outward, hinting at something left unsaid, a geographic
ellipsis. Pressed from behind by new cultures, new ideas,
a new religion, the Irish must have been tempted to probe
the mysterious west, first in story, then in the oxskin-cov-
ered crafts that they knew so well how to row and sail.
Story after story tells of adventurers who sailed west, the
sea a physical analogue for death. By Brendan's time,
monks seeking solitude had settled in the Hebrides, perhaps even the Orkneys, Shetlands, and Faeroes. Whether
these outermost isles were discovered by design or accident no one can say, but the pressure was clearly there to
explore the watery infinity, to find what lay beyond the
horizon both physically and spiritually.

Tim Severin provided a service to the world of ideas
when he took his skin boat across the Atlantic. It hardly
matters whether he was following Brendan's course or
not; to read Severin's account of his voyage is to gain a
vivid impression of what it meant to sail in the cold, gale-
swept North Atlantic in a craft of sticks and skins. We
know the Irish did it. There is evidence that they reached
Iceland before the Vikings. The North Atlantic climate
between the fifth and eighth centuries was milder than it
is today; still, on the face of Severin's experience, the Irish
voyages seem superhuman. The men who achieved these
epic journeys were Christians who ostensibly worshiped
a transcendent God, but their lives were lived up to their
necks in the immanent. And in mystery.

MYSTERY, BUT NOT MIRACLE. We have already seen
that early Irish Christians did not have much truck with

the miraculous, as evidenced, among other things, by that
most remarkable book of Augustinus Hibernicus on the
"miracles" of Scripture. In some ways, Augustinus is
closer in spirit to ourselves than to his contemporary theologians of the Continent. Closer to us in his admission
of ignorance and in his sense that God acts *within* the
nature of things and not in contradistinction to them.
Carey says of Augustinus: "Unlike the Fathers of the
Church, whose only concerns (and quite legitimately
so!) were the word of God and the souls of men, he
wished to comprehend the world for its own sake; the
universe for him was not a blank tablet on which God
could write whatever he pleased, but an intricate living
organism whose beauty and integrity were respected by
its Maker." Marina Smyth agrees: The early Irish
Christians had an "unabashed interest in the universe,"
she says—in Sun, Moon, stars, rainbows, tides, and
weather—that stands "in sharp contrast with the attitude of Saint Augustine [of Hippo], who pointed out . . .
that it is a waste of time to study such questions since
they are of no use in reaching blessedness."

The author of *On the Miracles of Holy Scripture,* the
Irish Augustine, had as his subject stories from the Middle East that had been defined as canonical, indeed
divinely inspired, by the Roman Church. These stories
tell of a creation in time not so long ago, of the corruption
of nature by Original Sin, and of God's miraculous interventions in a world—all of which runs counter to what
we know of druidic tradition. In the sacred traditions of
the Celtic fringe, the universe's past recedes into the mists
of prehistory, all of nature is infused with divinity, and
nothing happens that is not part of the nature of things.

Augustinus Hibernicus gamely struggled to reconcile the two traditions, with sometimes ludicrous results.

In fact, the two traditions are difficult to mesh. Nature cannot be both fallen and sacred. Either miraculous transgressions of natural law occur, or they do not. God cannot be Wholly Other and immanent in creation. Augustinus was not the first to try to reconcile these contradictory streams of thought. We still try to reconcile them today, in the so-called war of religion and science. But the battle is not between religion and science; it is between two individually inadequate worldviews, which might be called *mystery without science* and *science without mystery*. Augustinus, too, was caught in a bind. He was steeped in the pantheistic worldview of the Celtic fringe but called by Christian orthodoxy to Rome. He twists and turns with remarkable agility, but in the end he is left hanging in the wind.

It is in this context that we must understand Brendan's voyage, whether it was a historical reality or merely stands in for the outward migrations of the early Irish clerics. The western voyages of discovery are heterodox by their very nature, thrusting outward from Rome, probing the unknown, driven by curiosity. The truth is always *just there*, over the horizon. Heaven is not an abstruse abstraction, above and beyond this imperfect world; heaven is *out there*, beyond the mists and winds and ice. The Land of Delight is not outside of the world but in it, to be achieved not by leaving the flesh behind (immaterial immortal souls, not bodies, were the concern of the Roman Church, as the Inquisition later made horrendously clear, and this in spite of that most curious and improbable doctrine, the postapocalypse resurrection of bodies) but by living fully in the here and now. It is almost certain that the Irish monks reached Iceland, perhaps Greenland, perhaps even beyond. However far they got, they were driven by the same motivations that inspired Tim Severin to follow in a boat that everyone said would break up in the first storm: to challenge orthodoxy, to know, and to live as fully as possible in the body of the world.

THE FAIRY PEOPLE OF DRUIDIC tradition no longer satisfy our rational needs. The pantheon of Greco-Roman gods have been sent packing too. The eminent biologist Edward O. Wilson says of the pagan gods: "The spirits our ancestors knew intimately fled first the rocks and trees, then the distant mountains. Now they are in the stars, where their final extinction is possible. *But we cannot live without them.* People need a sacred narrative." And he is right. The human mind cannot live without mystery. Reason alone will not satisfy. Science without awe is sterile. A life lived without praise and thanksgiving is a shabby sort of life indeed. The cultural historian (and Roman Catholic priest) Thomas Berry agrees: The so-called antagonisms between science and faith are deeper than they appear to be, he says. The ancient Christian creation story has functioned well in its institutional and moral efficiency, but it is no longer relevant; it simply does not meet the most basic tests of rational knowing. But the newer, scientific story of creation has not yet acquired a spiritual aspect. "An integral story has not emerged," he writes.

Berry urges us to assimilate the scientific story of creation—what he calls the New Story—into our religious and prayerful lives: "The universe, the solar system,

and the planet earth in themselves and in their evolutionary emergence constitute for the human community the
primary revelation of that ultimate mystery whence all
things emerge into being." The forms of religious belief
that guided us in the past are inadequate to energize
our future, he says.

For Berry, the spiritual significance of the New Story,
the scientific story, is this: The universe is a unity—an
interacting, evolving, and genetically related community
of beings bound together inseparably in space and time.
Our responsibilities to each other and to all of creation
are implicit in this unity. Each of us is profoundly impli-
cated in the functioning and fate of every other being on
the planet, and ultimately, perhaps, throughout the universe. What Berry asks for is a faith not unlike what I
have found on the mountain, as expressed in the
thoughts and actions of the early Irish Christians.

So far, scientists have resisted any attempt to infuse
their empirical enterprise with spiritual values. They
are fearful, and rightly so, of diluting a successful truth-
generating methodology with archaic "mysticism." With
creationists and New Agers storming the barricades of
science, intent on bringing down the walls, who can blame
scientists for jealously maintaining their aloof detachment
from spirituality? Meanwhile, the majority of people recoil
from the scientific story of the world, which they see as
cold and forbidding, and instead seek comfort in an older,
more human-centered cosmology—a cosmology of miracles and redemption by a loving (or just) personal God
lodged outside of the creation who listens and responds to
our prayers. What is the alternative? In the new scientific
spirituality, as embraced by Berry and increasing numbers

of others, God is revealed in and through the creation, as law and chaos, light and darkness, creator and destroyer, animating every aspect of the everyday world with mystery and meaning. In this we are close in spirit to the early Christian Irish of the Atlantic fringe.

All cultures, everywhere on Earth, have stories, passed down in sacred writings or tribal myths, that answer the questions: Where did the world come from? What is our place in it? What is the source of order and disorder? What will be the fate of the world and of ourselves? The human mind demands—requires—answers to these questions. The story cycles of the pre-Christian Irish, and of the pre-Celtic peoples of Ireland, supplied answers. The Bible and the Church Fathers supplied answers. And the scientific tradition has answers too. The scientific story, the New Story (as Berry calls it), is the product of thousands of years of human curiosity, observation, experimentation, and creativity. It is an evolving story, not yet finished. Perhaps it will never be finished. It is a story that begins with an explosion from a seed of infinite energy. The seed expands and cools. Particles form, then atoms of hydrogen and helium. Stars and galaxies coalesce from swirling gas. Stars burn and explode, forging heavy elements—carbon, nitrogen, oxygen—and hurling them into space. New stars are born, with planets made of heavy elements. On one planet near a typical star in a typical galaxy life appears in the form of microscopic self-replicating ensembles of atoms. Life evolves, over billions of years, resulting in ever more complex organisms. Continents move. Seas rise and fall. The ice advances and retreats. The atmosphere changes. Millions of species of life appear and become extinct. Others adapt, survive, and spill out progeny. At last, consciousness appears. One of the millions of species on the planet looks into the night sky or the limitless sea and wonders what it means, feels the spark of love, tenderness, and responsibility, makes up stories—of Cu Chulainn, Fionn Mac Cumhail, Oisin and Niamh, of Adam, Eve, and the Serpent, of the man of Nazareth who was crucified and rose from the dead, eventually making up the New Story, the scientific story of creation.

The New Story has important advantages over all the stories that have gone before. For one thing, it works. It works so well that it has become the irreplaceable basis of technological civilization. We test the story in every way we can devise, in its particulars and in its totality. For example, we build giant particle accelerating machines to see what happened in the first hot moments of the Big Bang. We put telescopes into space to look for the radiation of the primeval explosion. With spectroscopes and radiation detectors we analyze the composition of stars and galaxies and compare them to our theories for the origin of the world. Always and in every way we try to prove the story wrong. When the story fails, we change it.

Although primarily an invention of Western culture, the New Story has become the story of all educated peoples throughout the world. There is no such thing as European science, Chinese science, Navajo science; scientists of all cultures, religions, and political persuasions exchange ideas freely and apply the same criteria of verification and falsification. Like most children, I was taught that my story was the "true story," and that all others were false, or at best (like the Irish myth of Oisin and Niamh) sweet fairy tales. Sometimes our so-called true stories gave us permission to hurt those who lived by other stories. But in a world of international air travel, instant exchange of information, and weapons of mass destruction, we can no longer afford to squabble over which of our many stories is true. The New Story, by its universality, helps put the old animosities behind us.

Some of the old stories, such as the one I was taught as a child, placed the essence of our humanity—our "immortal souls"—outside of space and time and gave us dominion over the millions of other creatures of the Earth. The New Story places us squarely in a cosmic unfolding of space and time and teaches our biological affinity to all humanity and other creatures. We are inextricably related to all of life, to the planet itself, and even to the lives of stars. The microbiologist Ursula Goodenough, in her book *The Sacred Depths of Nature,* reminds us that the word *religion* derives from the Latin *religio*, "to bind together again." She writes: "We have throughout the ages sought connection with higher powers in the sky or beneath the earth, or with ancestors living in some other realm. We have also sought, and found, religious fellowship with one another. And now we realize that we are connected to all creatures. Not just in food chains or ecological equilibria. We share a common ancestor. . . . We share evolutionary constraints and possibilities. We are connected all the way down."

No omniscient deity intervenes at will in the creation, answers prayers, or leads all things to a predetermined end. The New Story asserts our responsibility for our own lives and the future of the planet. We find ourselves alone, in a universe of unanticipated complexity, beauty, and dimension, with an awesome responsibility to use our gifts wisely.

We treasure the ancient stories for the wisdom and values they teach us. We praise the creation in whatever poetic languages and rituals our traditional cultures have taught us. But only the New Story has the global authority to help us navigate the future. It is not the "true" story, but it is certainly the truest. Of all the stories, it is the only one that has had its feet held to the fire of exacting empirical experience.

FROM THE TOP OF MOUNT Brandon the New Story unfolds all around me. In the crush of continents that heaved the mountains skyward. In the shaping of the hills by glaciers. In the tumbling atmosphere, stirred into motion by the spinning Earth. In the single-celled algae that grow in Saint Brendan's well (our bodies are, in a sense, colonies of amoebas). In the vast bowl of the sea that draws our imagination westward, and in the water itself, cradle of life, forged in starry nebula, gathered by gravity with the body of the Earth. "I am the meaning of the poem," sings Amergin. "I am the god that makes fire in the head."

What is our response to such a universe, to such a God, immanent in every particle of creation, hidden in our infinite ignorance, knowable only through a glass darkly, the Deus Absconditus of the mystics, the absconded deity? In this too the monks and holy women of Brendan's generation have much to teach us, and to learn their lesson we must go to their places of prayer. But before we descend the mountain, let us turn one last time to John Carey, and what he says we might learn from the early Irish Christians: "Existence itself, then, is the ultimate miracle: had our eyes not grown so dull, they would be dazzled with ineffable wonder wherever we turned our gaze."

GALLARUS
A NEST BESIDE THY ALTAR

Gallarus Oratory in County Kerry

WHEN TWO PAGAN PRINCESSES, daughters of King Laoghaire, asked Patrick about his God, he is said to have answered: "Our God is the God of all things, the God of the sky and earth, the God of sea and stream, the God of sun and moon, the God of the great high mountains and the deep glens, the God of heaven, in heaven and under heaven. And he has a household— heaven and earth and the sea and all they contain." From what we know of the druidic faith of the Celts, none of this would have sounded particularly foreign to the princesses. Indeed, Patrick's words evoke nothing so much as the poem of Amergin, that primary document of Irish literature. Most notably different about Patrick's faith, I suppose, would be the sidelining of the fairy folk in favor of a single personal deity, although the fairy folk lingered long in the Irish subpantheon, accompanied by an overlay of Christian saints and angels.

Writing about Celtic spirituality, Noel Dermot O'Donoghue speaks of the Irish perception of a *Presence* in the world, existing somewhere between light and darkness, clarity and mystery, matter and spirit, a Presence that inhabits what O'Donoghue calls the "imaginal" world (as opposed to "imaginary"). The God of the earliest Irish Christians was the king of the elements,

Righ na nDúl, he says, and adds: "Just as Christianity became wedded to *logos* in Hellenism, and to authority in Romanism, it became wedded to nature and the natural world, in all its various levels and regions, in the Celtic world."

What does it mean to honor a God whose immanence takes precedence over his transcendence? How do we worship a God who animates all things but reveals nothing directly of himself? And, most important from a modern point of view, how do we pray to a deity who eludes even the personal pronouns (*he* or *she, himself* or *herself*), who absconds from the temples of our imagination and hides in the interstices of creation? If the mystery and majesty of nature creates "a fire in the head," as it must inevitably for anyone who thinks deeply about the world, to whom or to what do we address our fevered response? Is any sort of prayer compatible with the New Story, the scientific story of creation?

There is a tradition of Christian prayer that is open to mystery and yet attuned to God's immanence. The Trappist contemplative Thomas Merton describes it this way: "When I am liberated by silence, when I am no longer involved in the measurement of life, but in the living of it, I can discover a form of prayer in which there is effectively no distraction. My whole life becomes a prayer. My whole silence is full of prayer. . . . Let me seek, then, the gift of silence, and poverty, and solitude, where everything I touch is turned into prayer: where the sky is my prayer, the birds are my prayer, the wind in the trees is my prayer, for God is all in all." He might have added: *The whirling galaxies are my prayer. The ceaselessly weaving DNA is my prayer. The folding of the mountains and the grinding glaciers are my prayer.* The more fully we grasp the *realness* of the world, the more fully are these things the objects of our contemplation, praise, thanksgiving.

Merton defines monastic prayer as "a prayer of silence, simplicity, contemplative and meditative unity, a deep personal integration in an attentive, watchful listening of 'the heart.'" And surely this kind of prayer was practiced by the Irish monks who lived on the rocky fringe of Europe, in places of such stark solitude that even today we are moved by the rigor of their lives. On the bleak vertical rock of Skellig Michael, an island in the Atlantic near the end of the Dingle Peninsula, is a cluster of half a dozen tiny "beehive" huts that for centuries housed a community of monks—cold, dank structures more like caves than proper habitations. The monastery, such as it is, is perched precariously on a narrow ledge high above the sea. There is hardly a patch of fertile soil (at least not until the monks created a few terraced gardens with seaweed and sand), no spring of freshwater, no landing place sheltered from the fury of the sea. The monks lived on the flesh of birds, eggs, fish. There could have been very little cooking or fire for warmth; not a tree or bush grows on the island, nor is there a single clod of combustible turf. Perhaps the monks grew vegetables in their tiny terraced plots, in soil laboriously manufactured from whatever organic substance they could scrape together. They drank rainwater collected in the hollows of the rocks. On those few days of the year when the sea permitted, they were presumably supplied from the mainland with butter, dried meat, and vegetables. Why would anyone subject himself to such a life? Not even the most rigorous of modern monastic disciplines begins to approach the bleak hardship of life on the Skellig.

But there is beauty too, and grandeur. Everyone who goes to the Skellig falls under its spell. The black rock rises from the sea as if it were the first thrust of the creation itself, a tentative emergence of order from chaos, God's cautious finger to the wind. For a people who believed (with Patrick, Brendan, and Columbanus) in a God of sky and earth, sea and stream, Sun and Moon, mountains and glens, the Skellig must have seemed the very vestibule of heaven. I like to suppose that the monks who lived there were liberated by solitude and silence, no longer involved in the measurement of life but in the living of it. They gathered in their minuscule oratory for formal collective prayer, but every action, every sense impression, every turn of thought, was, by Thomas Merton's definition, an act of praise. In her wonderful book, *A Natural History of the Senses*, Diane Ackerman speaks of perception—the mental registration of sense impressions—as a form of grace. In Roman Catholic theology one must be disposed to grace to receive it, which means (in Ackerman's metaphor) living with the five windows of the senses thrown open to the world, uncurtained, in all weathers. She writes, "Life showers over everything, radiant, gushing." The monks of Skellig sought a place where the rush and gush of nature were unceasing. We know from the texts that have come down to us from their time that what the monks sought was contained in the pre-Christian concept of *neart*—a strength, power, or force that animates the world. The winds of the Atlantic played over their heartstrings like Aeolian harps. Their lives give new meaning to the phrase "living on the edge."

There are similar monastic establishments on islands all up and down the Irish coast, although none has been so well preserved—by its inaccessibility!—as the monastery on Skellig Michael. The men who built these refuges did not surrender the life of the mind for their rugged physical solitude; they were scholarly, inquisitive, in some ways more curious about the ancient empirical learning of the Mediterranean than their continental counterparts. According to legend, Brendan prepared for his voyage of discovery by retreating to a hermitage on Mount Brandon's summit, but he was apparently a knowledgeable seaman too, acquainted with winds and currents, the arts of celestial navigation, and tales of earlier excursions upon the Western Sea: Phoenician sorties, perhaps, and fragmentry reports from sailors who had been blown by unpredictable winds onto island shores—the Shetlands, the Faeroes, the Azores—and returned. Brendan, and other Irish men and women of his time, merged the intellectual abstractions of Mediterranean Christianity with druidic nature worship to forge a way of living that honored the mind as it listened with the heart, firmly and exuberantly *in the world* but always aware of an Unspeakable that infuses all things with mystery.

ON THE SKELLIG, several of the monks' cells survived intact into our own time, but the community's tiny rectangular oratory (place of prayer) is roofless. Of all the places Irish men and women built for prayer before the coming of the Vikings in the ninth century, only one remains intact. At Gallarus, on the Dingle Peninsula west of Mount Brandon is a structure that must be counted as one of the most remarkable in all of Ireland, even in all of Europe: the Gallarus Oratory. The building is about the size of a one-car garage, rectangular in plan, in the shape of an overturned boat. It is built of unmortared stone, beautifully fitted together, with corbeled side walls about a yard thick curving upward until they meet at the ridge line. A small trapezoidal opening at the front may have once been closed by a door of leather or wood; an adult must stoop to enter. A tiny arched window at the rear admits a shaft of light into the gloom. The structure is as weathertight today as when it was built.

Everyone who sees the Gallarus Oratory for the first time is stunned into silence. They have never seen anything like it, and never will. Inexplicably, almost miraculously, it has survived the ravages of time, in particular the predations of farmers seeking building stone. There are other structures like it on the Dingle Peninsula, but all exist only in fragments; the Gallarus Oratory has the look of a building that was constructed yesterday. Exactly how old it is no one can say. Some evidence from the site suggests the oratory was built in the century or so after Saint Brendan's death in 577. But the building is so carefully and beautifully made that some archaeologists propose a later date, perhaps as a second structure on an older site. In any case, it is almost certain that the building was in place before the Vikings came ravaging along this coast in the year 850, when they plundered the monastery on Skellig Michael (though what they found to plunder in that desolate place is a mystery).

The Gallarus Oratory stands within a roughly circular stone-walled enclosure, divided across by a wall as by a diameter. Not much has been done at Gallarus by way of archaeological excavation, but the site is similar to one at Reask a few miles away, a Christian settlement of the fifth to twelfth centuries that has been extensively excavated. Reask is also enclosed by an oval wall, with an internal wall separating the secular from the sacred precincts of the community. In the secular area there are foundations of the circular stone habitations characteristic of the Dingle Peninsula—thick windowless rubble walls a yard or two high, which were presumably roofed over with timber and thatch. There are paved paths and drains. Domestic artifacts found by the archaeologists include glass beads, spindle whorls, and quern stones. Furnace pits and slag heaps give evidence of iron working, and fragments of crucibles indicate bronze or glass work. A corn-drying kiln adds an element of agriculture. All in all, we can imagine a small community busy with the business of everyday life, living in some peril from domestic and foreign predators. But clearly religion was the overarching concern for whoever lived at Reask. Even before the archaeological excavations the site had been known for its magnificently carved cross slab, standing about as high as a man, decorated with a circled Maltese cross, a pattern of elaborate spirals, and the letters *DNE* (*domine*, Lord). Other beautiful cross stones have been excavated at Reask. Central to the sacred precinct is the foundation of a small rectangular oratory.

Except for the overlay of Christian worship, the settlement at Reask is not dissimilar to the circular "ring forts" of earth or stone that were a characteristic feature of this landscape long before Saint Patrick set foot in Ireland. About 450 ring forts have been recorded in the Dingle Peninsula. They were primarily domestic in nature, the mostly earthen walls serving to enclose animals and perhaps provide some protection from wolves. At least a third of the ring forts have been destroyed by farmers in modern times by being incorporated into fields, but in their collectivity they remain an impressive geographic presence, and it is easy to see how in the imaginations of country people they became "fairy forts" or "fairy circles," places where the displaced spirits of the pagan deities lived and held court. Had it not been for fear of disturbing a sacred presence in the land, it is likely that many more of these sites would have been lost to agriculture.

For centuries the ring forts were protected by fear of the fairies; now they are protected by law. The ancient monuments of the Irish countryside stood in most danger of destruction during a brief twentieth-century window of time between the long sway of fairy myth and the dawn of ecological consciousness. It is easy to dismiss the fairy tales as superstition, but they are more than superstition. They are a remnant of druidic pantheism, an anthropomorphic manifestation of the Celtic sense that all of nature is imbued with *neart*, powers and forces we don't fully understand. This is not so different from our modern ecological consciousness of the intrinsic value of all things in a landscape, including the historical artifacts—the ring forts and standing stones—that are part of the human landscape. Celtic *neart* and scientific ecology are two sides of the same coin.

For centuries, the two great enemies of the landscape were a religion—continental Christianity—that preached the fallen state of nature, on the one hand, and an exaggerated Enlightenment rationalism that saw nature as little more than an object for dispassionate investigation ("We murder to dissect," complained Wordsworth), on the other. The archaeological artifacts of the Dingle Peninsula survived as well as they did because here continental Christianity was mitigated with a healthy dose of Celtic pantheism, and because, later, the Irish Church vigorously resisted incursions of Enlightenment thought into Irish life. Today in Ireland, the ancient Celtic sense that all of nature is sacred has been revived as a post-Christian ecological consciousness. The enemy of the landscape is now neither religion nor scientism, but greed.

PERHAPS THE GALLARUS ORATORY SURVIVED because it early became and remained a place of pilgrimage, or perhaps because even from earliest times people recognized it as something of an architectural masterpiece. The oratory, as its name implies, was meant for prayer, and one cannot enter that cool darkness without feeling a sense of mystery that provokes a contemplative response. What sort of prayer took place in the cool cave of the Gallarus Oratory no one can say at this remove. Perhaps a tiny oil lamp flickered in the waxy darkness. Was there an altar against the back wall? Surely no seats or benches in this restricted space. It is hard to imagine an exuberant congregation singing a *Te Deum*—the voices crushed back to earth by the weight of the corbeled stone. Rather, one imagines a single person, or two, or three, prostrate in the dark, praying as Thomas Merton defined monastic prayer: *A silent listening of the heart.*

I was raised in a culture of prayer; it permeated every aspect of my young life. The school day began and ended with prayer. As an altar boy at our parish church, I served countless masses, benedictions, weddings, funerals. A not insignificant proportion of my youth was spent in church, listening to prayers, reciting prayers. Yet, looking back on my childhood, I wonder what it all meant. Most of the prayers I recited were formalistic; I might as well have been mumbling the Pledge of Allegiance to the Flag or nursery rhymes. Many of the prayers were in Latin and therefore doubly inscrutable. Certainly, there was nothing spontaneous or heartfelt about my prayers. The only prayers that were not formalistic were anxious petitions: *Dear God, let me do well on my spelling test; let me get the bike for my birthday; let the toothache go away.* In these earnest entreaties to a deity, I was not alone. A recent *Newsweek* magazine poll found that 87 percent of Americans believe in a God who hears and answers prayers, and more than a quarter of Americans pray to such a God every day. For many people, the entire purpose of prayer is to invoke God's intervention in the course of their daily lives, to adjust the tilt of the universe in their personal favor, to redirect the stream of time ever so marginally so that benefices flow their way.

As a scientist, I have examined the evidence for the efficacy of petitionary prayer, and found none. Yes, every person who prays has anecdotal evidence for efficacy, mistaking coincidence for causality. But every double-blind experiment done in a medical context to test the efficacy of intercessory prayer has yielded negative results. The so-called miracles—the collections of abandoned crutches at Marian shrines, for example—turn to smoke when examined one by one. I am now more interested in the kind of prayer I found on the mountain. If we accept, with the early Irish saints, God's immanence, prayer becomes an expression of wonder, thanksgiving, and praise, not to someone *outside* of the creation who could and might intervene to redirect the flow of events, but to the creative agency *within* the creation—a God whom we intuit through the mind and heart but who evades all definitions (including the convenient pronoun *who*).

A COROLLARY OF BELIEF IN the efficacy of petitionary prayer is the so-called problem of evil: If God can redirect the flow of events in contravention of natural law, why does a loving and just God allow bad things to happen to good people? Theologians have wrestled with this difficulty from time immemorial, without satisfactory resolution. But a resolution is hinted at in the Celtic notion of God's immanence. "I am the point of the spear," sang Amergin. He might have added, *I am the wind that blows the ship upon the rocks, I am the wolf that carries the lamb from the fold, I am the pestilence that takes the child from the parent.* The creation and the Creator are all of a piece: light and darkness, happiness and sorrow, life and death. Eriugena was an Irish monk who taught at the court of Charlemagne's grandson Charles the Bald, and who carried to the Continent some of the theology of the Celtic fringe. He wrote: "We should not think of God and of the creature as two different things remote from one another, but as one and the same. For not only does the creature subsist in God, but God, in a wonderful and ineffable way, is created in the creature." It is a dazzling formulation, which removes (or at least mitigates) the problem of evil. Of course, Eriugena's formulation was officially condemned by the Church after his death as excessively pantheistic. By then the continental Church had committed itself to transcendence and to miracles—

that is, to a theology that removed God from the everyday and placed him outside of nature.

For Eriugena, our personal redemption and the redemption of the world are one. When we recognize this, a responsibility for all of creation falls upon our shoulders. God does not let bad things happen to good people, but we sometimes do. The creation is neither good nor evil, but Jesus of Nazareth and other great religious leaders have emphasized our freedom to act in ways that can nudge history toward the good. What Celtic pantheism advantageously received from Christianity is the Sermon on the Mount, and indeed the entire message of the gospels: *Do unto others as you would have them do unto you.* In the broadest sense of this maxim we recognize an ecological wholeness, a basis for moral action in the world, and a concept of redemption in which our every action moves all of creation toward harmony. In the words of the Eighty-fourth Psalm: *Even the sparrow finds a home, and the swallow a nest, where she rears her brood beside thy altars.*

A FEW YEARS AGO, I spent a night in the Gallarus Oratory. I can't say exactly why I went there late in the evening, or why I intended to sit up all night unsleeping in that dark space. I suppose I wanted to experience something of whatever it was that inspired Irish men and women to seek out these rough hermitages on the edge of civilization. They were, to be sure, pilgrims of the Absolute, seeking their God in a raw, ecstatic encounter with stone, wind, sea, and sky. The oratory is today something of a tourist mecca, but at night the place is isolated and dark, far from human habitation. From the door of the oratory, one looks down a sloping mile of fields to the twinkling lights of the village of Ballydavid on Smerwick Harbor.

The Sun had long set when I arrived at Gallarus, although at Ireland's latitude the twilight in summer never quite fades from the northern horizon. It was a moonless night, ablaze with stars, Jupiter brightest of all. Meteors occasionally streaked the sky, and satellites cruised more stately orbits. Inside the oratory, I snuggled into a back corner, tucked my knees under my chin, and waited. The darkness was palpable, pungent; "like going into a turfstack," says Seamus Heaney in a poem on Gallarus. I could see nothing but the starlit outline of the door, not even my hand in front of my face. The silence was broken only by the *swish-swish* of my own breath. As the hours passed, I began to feel a presence, a powerful sensation of something or someone sharing that empty darkness. I am not, as you surely know by now, a mystical person, but I *knew* that I was not alone, and I could imagine those hermit monks of the seventh century sharing the same intense conviction of "someone in the room." At last, I was spooked to the point that I abandoned my interior corner and went outside.

A night of exceptional clarity. Stars spilling into the sea. And in the north, as if as a reward for my lonely vigil, the aurora borealis—the northern lights—danced toward the zenith. How can I describe what I saw? Rays of silver light streaming up from the sea, as if from some enchanted Oz just over the horizon. Shimmering columns of fairy radiance, black night made suddenly phosphorescent. The aurora is caused by high-energy electrons and protons, hurled from the Sun by massive magnetic storms on its surface; several days later, this solar wind of particles slams into the Earth's magnetic field, sculpting and shaping it, drawing it out into a long tail that points away from the Sun. The magnetic field in turn snares electrons from the wind and pumps them inward along lines of magnetic influence. Down they dive, near the poles of the Earth, smashing into the rarefied air of the upper atmosphere, causing the atoms of the atmosphere to glow like the gas in a neon tube. Photographs of the Earth from space show the planet permanently capped with a crown of light, at least where a pole resides in darkness. On almost any clear, dark night near the Arctic and Antarctic Circles the lights might be seen. Only occasionally, during particularly violent solar storms, does the aurora push down into the latitudes of Ireland. Our knowledge of the aurora and its causes was not complete until the dawn of the space age, when rockets probed the upper atmosphere and measured the fluxes of solar particles spiraling up and down along lines of magnetic force. The lights in the sky are the signature of the magnetic and material entanglement of Earth and Sun, the luminous badge of our place in the cosmos near a turbulent star.

As I watched from the doorway of the Gallarus Oratory, I remembered something the nineteenth-century explorer Charles Francis Hall wrote while watching the aurora from the Arctic: "My first thought was, 'Among the gods there is none like unto Thee, O Lord; neither are there any works like unto thy works!' . . . We looked, we SAW, we TREMBLED." Hall knew he was watching a natural physical phenomenon, not a miracle, but his reaction suggests the power of the aurora even on a mind trained in the methods of science. What, then, did the monks of Gallarus think of the aurora, thirteen hundred years ago, as they wrestled to understand exceptional phenomena? Miracle or *neart*? An intervention of a transcendent God who exists outside of creation, or the manifestation of a power and force that resides in every star, stone, and blade of grass? Stepping out from the inky darkness of their stone chapel, they must surely have felt that the shimmering columns of light were somehow meant for them alone, a gift or a revelation. And perhaps in a way they were right. After all, they had placed themselves in circumstances where they might encounter the majesty and beauty of nature—something we seldom do in our increasingly virtual lives.

We have left the age of miracles behind, but not, let us hope, our sense of wonder. Our quest for encounter with the Absolute goes arm in arm with our study of nature. The great Jesuit paleontologist Teilhard de Chardin celebrated scientific knowledge of the world as a basis for prayer. "Let us go on and on endlessly increasing our perception of the hidden powers that slumber, and the infinitesimally tiny ones that swarm about us, and the immensities that escape us simply because they appear as a point," he wrote, extolling the atomic and the galactic. Each discovery plunges us a little deeper into the ground of all Mystery, he believed, leading us at last into contemplation of the ineffable, unspeakable deity who "through his Spirit stirs up into a ferment the mass of the universe." Less and less, he said near the end of his life, did he discern a difference between research and adoration.

Like Teilhard, we are pilgrim scientists, perched on the edge of knowing, curious and attentive. The Gallarus Oratory was built for prayer at a time when the world was thought to be charged with the active spirit of the Creator: Every zephyr blew good or ill; springs flowed or dried up at the deity's whim; lights danced in a predawn sky as blessings or portents. Today, we know that the lights dance for reasons that have nothing to do with our supplications or with a deity's willfulness; electrons crash down from the Sun, igniting luminescence. But our response to the lights might be prayerful, nonetheless: wonder, thanksgiving, praise. If we are attentive and knowledgeable, the lights will lead us into encounter with the ineffable Spirit that stirs the universe into a ferment.

As the Sun brightened the eastern sky and the last shreds of aurora faded, I was suddenly startled by a pair of swallows that began to dart in and out of the Gallarus Oratory, hunting insects on the wing. I followed them inside and discovered a nest with three chicks perched on a protruding stone just above the place I had been sitting. The mysterious presence I had felt so strongly in the darkness was not a god, nor fairy spirit, nor angel, nor demon, but the respirations and featherings of swallows.

JUST OVER THE HILL FROM my Irish cottage is another early ecclesiastical site associated by tradition with the grave of Saint Manchan: an oratory similar to that at Gallarus, although less well preserved, several inscribed crosses, and a holy well. In the eighteenth and nineteenth centuries the well was the venue for a popular "pattern," or ritual, a kind of semipagan devotion during which participants circled the well sunwise seven times while reciting the prayers of the rosary; sometimes pebbles or berries were thrown in the well, one for each time around. The pattern was followed by music and dancing at the crossroads; sometimes a fiddler or a piper from Dingle played, or sometimes (so poor were the participants) the dancing was conducted to whistling or humming—"puss music," it was called. The more secular aspects of these celebrations came under attack from the clergy, who did their best to make certain that the faithful remained unattached to the pleasures of this world. Father John Casey, a nineteenth-century parish priest of nearby Ballyferriter, was a stern enemy of fiddlers and pipers. On one occasion when Casey found music being played, he took hold of the piper, kicked and cuffed him unmercifully, and smashed his pipes before the dismayed assembly. Such was the fate of those of the faithful who let their prayerful assemblies partake of anything resembling the sensual or worldly. Some patterns in Ireland continue even to this day, at various holy wells and shrines, but by the middle of the twentieth century the associated secular entertainments had been suppressed.

Father Casey's gloomy appraisal of the physical world was characteristic of the culture I was brought up in by priests and nuns of the Irish diaspora. The world is a distraction from the true object of your piety, they said. If you would know God, you must shut the windows of your senses and listen to his voice. He will speak to you not through touch, taste, smell, sight, and sound but through the spirit, they said. So I closed my eyes and listened. And indeed I heard a voice, the insistent voice of the idling brain, easily mistaken for the whisper of God, but more likely the murmurings of self. It is no bad thing, I suppose, to listen to the voice of self. The self is a proper object of attention, for if there are mysteries in the world deserving of our contemplation, among the greatest of these is self. It is perhaps not surprising that so many people understand God as a person, for if it is the murmurings of self that we interpret as God's voice, it is certainly the voice of a person we hear.

Let us listen again to the "Song of Amergin," sometimes called "The Mystery," supposedly the first verses made in Ireland, in a time before Patrick and Brendan.

> *I am the wind on the sea.*
> *I am the ocean wave.*
> *I am the sound of the billows.*
> *I am the seven-horned stag.*
> *I am the hawk on the cliff.*
> *I am the dewdrop in sunlight.*
> *I am the fairest of flowers.*
> *I am the raging boar.*
> *I am the salmon in the deep pool.*
> *I am the lake on the plain.*
> *I am the meaning of the poem.*
> *I am the point of the spear.*
> *I am the god that makes fire in the head.*
> *Who levels the mountain?*
> *Who speaks the age of the moon?*
> *Who has been where the sun sleeps?*
> *Who, if not I?*

The poem has been discussed endlessly by scholars, as to its origin, translation, and meaning, but the secret of its appeal remains elusive. The simplicity of the poem belies its power to touch our hearts. Certainly, the simplicity is part of the poem's meaning. It affirms something that we all know, even if we cannot put our knowledge into words. Something that exists beyond words, beyond philosophy, beyond science. Something we can intuit—in silent, jubilant beholding—but not express. Something hidden deeply in the exquisite complexity of the world.

It is the thing that Thomas Merton draws our attention to in his discussion of prayer, in particular what he calls "prayer of the heart." He writes: "In the 'prayer of the heart' we seek first of all the deepest ground of our identity in God. We do not reason about dogmas of faith, or 'the mysteries.' We seek rather to gain a direct existential grasp, a personal experience of the deepest truths of life and faith, *finding ourselves in God's truth*." We discern this truth in direct and simple attention to *reality*, he says. Prayer is the yearning of the human heart for God's simple presence, for a personal understanding of our place in the picture, for a renunciation of all deluded images of ourselves, all exaggerated estimates of our own importance and capacities. "It is thus something much more than uttering petitions for good things external to our own deepest concerns," says Merton.

Apprehension of the wind on the sea, the ocean wave, the sound of the billows can be the highest kind of prayer if, as Merton suggests, our attention is directed to the real, the tangible, the immediately present. We are struck by the apprehension, rung like a bell. Color, shape, texture, matter, animation: stag, cliff, sunlight, spear. Not necessarily a mighty trumpet blast that shatters the walls of Jericho. Not a fiery cross in the sky. Not Lazarus rising from the dead. Rather, a gentle breeze. The croak of a raven in a mountain corrie. A blossom of pink thrift on a bare mountaintop. The prayer of the heart is not garrulous . . . It listens in silence, expectant.

And here we discern the twofold nature of attentive prayer: It is rooted in knowledge, enriched by reliable scientific knowledge of the world, but it goes beyond knowledge. John Cassian, an early Christian writer on monastic spirituality, describes something he calls *oratio ignita* (fiery prayer): "[The] mind is illumined by the infusion of heavenly light, not making use of any human forms of speech but with all the powers gathered together in unity it pours itself forth copiously and cries out to God in a manner beyond expression, saying so much in a brief moment that the mind cannot relate to it afterwards with ease or even go over it again after returning to itself." Cassian's "heavenly light" is what we might call with the contemporary poet Mary Oliver "the light at the center of every cell," which now and forever evades the descriptions of the scientist. I don't mean to sound mystical; I am not talking of a hallucinogenic or "out-of-body" experience, or the revelation of a wholly-other deity. Rather, I am talking about those moments of singular insight that inevitably come to anyone who attends to the details of *here* and *now*—to mystics, poets, and, yes, scientists.

I don't pretend to the insights of a Thomas Merton or a Teilhard de Chardin. I am an ordinary pilgrim, relearning to pray. I struggle to shed the shabby shawl of petitionary and formulaic prayer that I inherited as a child—to reject the default syllables "Me, Lord, Me"—so that I might attend to *things*—to swallows and auroras—to the voice that whispers in *all* of creation, to the voice that *is* all of creation.

The other day I bicycled across the hill to the Gallarus Oratory, to visit again, in daylight, the place where I spent the night with swallows. Along a quiet lane I stopped to remove a pebble from my shoe. I put down the kickstand of the bike and plopped myself down in the hedgerow alongside the road. As I fumbled with my shoe, I suddenly recognized that I had chosen to sit in a place of exceptional botanical riches, a wild garden. Silently, outside of time, I recited a litany that might have been Amergin's: *Buttercup. Clover. Herb Robert. Speed-well. Fuchsia. Foxglove. Loosestrife. Bramble rose. Tick tre-foil. Vetch.* Clouds tumbled off the Atlantic. Shadows raced along the tarmac. A few raindrops fell onto my upturned face. Without any human form of speech, my heart had articulated a prayer to the hidden God.

ACKNOWLEDGMENTS

FOR THE MAJORITY OF MY ascents of Brandon, it has been my good luck to have had the company of Maurice Sheehy, a Dingle native who is broadly knowledgeable about the history, archaeology, and culture of the peninsula. I would not have climbed the mountain as often as I did had it not been for Maurice's inspiration and friendship, nor would I have learned as many of the mountain's secrets.

A hefty debt of gratitude goes to a man I have not met, a scholar of early Irish theological writing, John Carey of the National University of Ireland, Cork. Carey's published translations and analyses provided an important key to piecing together various themes of this book.

Maurice Sheehy, John Carey, Robert Kruse, and Bartley MacPhaidin generously read early drafts of the book and made valuable comments. Their assistance does not mean they agree with everything I have to say, and I am solely responsible for errors of fact or interpretation.

Living in the shadow of Brandon has been made more pleasurable by the company of friends: the entire Sheehy family; John Holstead, Stephanie Holstead, and their daughters, Rachel and Una; Philip, Barbara, Charlotte, Sebastian, and Felix Naughton; Jim Long and Nórín Crowley, and their children; Catherine Long and Danny McDonnell, now sadly departed and much missed; and all our other friends and neighbors of the Dingle Peninsula.

Once again it has been my good fortune to have had the superb assistance of Jackie Johnson, my editor at Walker & Company; her knack for knowing what works and what doesn't is unerring. George Gibson, my publisher, has been a loyal supporter of my work, and I greatly value his friendship. Julie Mashack, Marlene Tungseth, Vicki Haire, Krystyna Skalski, and all the wonderful people at Walker have been a delight to work with.

Lastly, my wife, Maureen, has been, as always, a perspicacious reader and critic of my work, as well as my best friend.

NOTES

1. Brandon: Between Heaven & Earth

3 *According to local tradition* . . . : Scholars of ancient Irish are more inclined to identify Bran's landing point with Stoove Point at the entrance of Lough Foyle in County Donegal.

3 *Was the branch of white blossoms* . . . : Niall Mac Coitir, *Irish Trees: Myth, Legends and Folklore* (Cork: Collins Press, 2003).

7 *An uneasy tension* . . . : For aspects of this description of Catholic and Protestant Christianity, I am indebted to my friend, the theologian Robert Kruse.

12 *Literary critic Marjorie Hope Nicolson* . . . : Majorie Hope Nicolson, *Mountain Gloom and Mountain Glory* (New York: Norton, 1959).

20 *"Are not the mountains, waves, and skies . . .":* George Gordon Byron, quoted in ibid., p. 14.

2. Cloghane: Twilight of the Gods

32 *The name of the festival may mean "bright fire":* The etymologies of both names, of the festival and the god, are matters of some dispute.

33 *The Irish historian Máire MacNeill* . . . : Máire MacNeill, *The Festival of Lughnasa* (Oxford: Oxford University Press, 1962).

39 *The dew of May Day dawn* . . . : Alwyn Rees and Brinley Rees, *Celtic Heritage* (London: Thames and Hudson, 1961), p. 345.

3. Faha: Land of Milk & Honey

52 *Gerald of Wales, who wrote* . . . : Gerald of Wales, *The History and Topography of Ireland* (London: Penguin, 1982), p. 53.

56 *The Fianna were Celtic warriors . . . :* Many versions of this tale exist. This common telling may have first appeared in the eighteenth century.

59 *. . . the apparent change in attitudes toward women:* This is not to say that the place of women in pre-Christian Celtic Ireland was any bed of roses, or that anything existed resembling gender parity. It is rather how women appear in storytelling that concerns me here.

59 *One medieval Irish text calls women "greedy" . . . :* John Carey, *King of Mysteries: Early Irish Religious Writings* (Dublin: Four Courts Press, 1998), p. 162.

59 *"The women of the world . . .":* Ibid., p. 206.

61 *Gerald of Wales . . . :* Gerald of Wales, *The History and Topography of Ireland,* p. 81.

61–62 *"Victorious Brigit . . .":* Carey, *King of Mysteries,* p. 164.

4. BINN NA PORT: THE WILD & THE HOLY

64 *In Ralph Horne's* Geological Guide *. . . :* Ralph R. Horne, *Geological Guide to the Dingle Peninsula* (Geological Survey of Ireland, 1976).

65 *Even the archaeologists . . . : Dingle Peninsula Archaeological Survey* (Ballyferriter: Oidhreacht Chorca Dhuibhne, 1986).

67 *Steve MacDonogh of Dingle . . . :* Steve MacDonogh, *The Dingle Peninsula: History, Folklore, Archeology* (Dingle: Brandon Press, 1993), pp. 209–11.

69 *Climatologists tell us . . . :* A. R. Orme, *Ireland* (Chicago: Aldine, 1970), pp. 43–49.

70–71 *"a rather weakened and gloomy . . .":* Dáithí Ó hÓgáin, *The Sacred Isle: Belief and Religion in Pre-Christian Ireland* (Woodbridge and Cork: Boydell Press and Collins Press, 1999), p. 31.

73 *Some archaeologists suggest . . . :* Ibid., pp. 45–48.

75 *"I am the wind on the sea . . .":* This version of the "Song of Amergin" draws upon several published translations, including those of Douglas Hyde and Thomas Kinsella, and the assistance of my Irish-speaking friend Maurice Sheehy. The evocative line "I am the god that makes fire in the head" has been challenged by

John Carey (private communication). Any translation is fraught with linguistic difficulties, and the poem as represented here must only be taken impressionistically.

78 *In his book on pre-Christian Ireland* . . . : Ó hÓgáin, *The Sacred Isle,* p. 3.

82 *Saint Columbanus, a contemporary of Brendan* . . . : Carey, *King of Mysteries,* p. 23.

5. Coumaknock: Mountain Gloom, Mountain Glory

90 *"Irish Christianity was a faith* . . .": Marina Smyth, *Understanding the Universe in Seventh-Century Ireland* (Woodbridge: Boydell Press, 1996), p. 307.

91 *"For mountains and high ground* . . .": Aristotle, *Meteorologica,* bk. 1, chap. 13.

93 *John Carey* . . . *has provided us with translations* . . . : Carey, *King of Mysteries,* p. 10.

93 *"a rich and equivocal mixture* . . .": Ibid., p. 18.

94–95 *Saint Columbanus asked in a sermon* . . . : John Carey, private communication.

95 *"must first review the natural world* . . .": Quoted in Jonathan M. Wooding, ed., *The Otherworld Voyage in Early Irish Literature* (Dublin: Four Courts Press, 2000), p. 194.

95 *"the full extravagent strangeness of existence"*: Carey, *King of Mysteries,* p. 23.

96 *"My King of mysteries, of fair fame* . . .": Ibid.

96–97 *"Earth felt the wound* . . .": John Milton, *Paradise Lost,* bk. 9, line 782–83.

97 *"Up through the riven rock* . . .": Dante, *Purgatorio,* canto, lines 31–51, in *Divine Comedy,* trans. J. B. Fletcher (New York, 1931).

97–98 *"Understanding the world's mysteries* . . .": Carey, *King of Mysteries,* p. 23.

99 *"particularly impressive* . . .": Carey, *King of Mysteries,* p. 51.

100 *"The human imagination, at its most primitive level* . . .": Ó hÓgáin, *The Sacred Isle,* p. 5.

103–104 *"In seventh-century Ireland . . ."*: Smyth, *Understanding the Universe,* p. 309.

6. SUMMIT: DISCOVERY OF IGNORANCE

106 *Spread out on a table by my desk . . .*: M. Pracht, *Geology of Dingle Bay* (Geological Survey of Ireland, 1996).

110–11 *"All hail, Sublimity! . . ."*: Alfred Lord Tennyson, quoted by Nicolson in *Mountain Gloom and Mountain Glory,* p. 371.

111 *"By the divine powers of the great God . . ."*: Carey, *King of Mysteries,* p. 41.

114 *"On us who saw . . ."*: Quoted by John McPhee in *Annals of the Former World* (New York: Farrar, Straus and Giroux, 1998), pp. 78–79.

115 *"The greatest of all the accomplishments . . ."*: Lewis Thomas, "Debating the Unknowable," *Atlantic Monthly,* July 1981, quoted by Timothy Ferris in *Coming of Age in the Milky Way* (New York: William Morrow, 1988), p. 383.

115 *"Our ignorance, of course . . ."*: Ferris, *Coming of Age,* p. 383.

116 *. . . what physicist Stephen Hawking has called . . .*: Stephen Hawking, *A Brief History of Time* (New York: Bantam Books, 1988), p. 175.

116 *"The more we learn about the world . . ."*: Karl Popper, *Conjectures and Refutations* (New York: Basic Books, 1968), p. 28.

117 *"The capacity to tolerate complexity . . ."*: Heinz Pagels, *Perfect Symmetry* (New York: Simon and Shuster, 1985), p. 370.

117 *"No thinking man or woman . . ."*: Ferris, *Coming of Age,* p. 384.

121–22 *"Let whoever desires true wisdom . . ."*: Carey, *King of Mysteries,* p. 23.

123 *"If then a man wishes to know . . ."*: G. S. M. Walker, ed., *Sancti Columbani* (Dublin, 1957; repr. 1970), pp. 64–65.

7. ATLANTIC: THE NEW STORY

126 *"His thoughts were evil . . ."*: Quoted by Thomas Owen Clancy in Wooding, *The Otherworld Voyage,* p. 202.

130 ... *the tenth-century manuscript account* ... : Although this is the earliest extant manuscript version, it may be based on even earlier written accounts. See David N. Dumville in Wooding, *The Otherworld Voyage,* pp. 120–32.

131 *His published account of the crossing* ... : Tim Severin, *The Brendan Voyage* (New York: McGraw-Hill, 1978).

132 *In his book on Celtic spirituality* ... : Seán Ó Duinn, *Where Three Streams Meet: Celtic Spirituality* (Dublin: Columba Press, 2000), p. 61.

133–34 *Another Irish Catholic priest ... calls his little book* ... : John J. Ó Ríordáin, *The Music of What Happens* (Dublin: Columba Press, 1996), pp. 109–10.

134 *Two strategies were employed* ... : John Carey, *A Single Ray of the Sun: Religious Speculation in Early Ireland* (Andover, Mass.: Celtic Studies Publications, 1999), p. 20.

137 *"Unlike the Fathers of the Church ..."*: Carey, ibid., p. 68.

137 *Marina Smyth agrees* ... : Smyth, *Understanding the Universe,* p. 305.

138 ... *or merely stands in for the outward migrations* ... : The *Navigatio* is also taken to be a metaphor for a spiritual journey, perhaps even the annual cycle of the liturgy.

139 *"The spirits of our ancestors ..."*: E. O. Wilson, *Consilience* (New York: Knopf, 1998), p. 264.

139 *"An integral story has not emerged ..."*: Thomas Berry, "The New Story: Comments on the Origin, Identification and Transmission of Values," *Teilhard Studies* 1, winter 1978.

143 *"We have throughout the ages sought ..."*: Ursula Goodenough, *The Sacred Depths of Nature* (New York: Oxford University Press, 1998), p. 73.

145 *"Existence itself ..."*: Carey, *A Single Ray of the Sun,* p. 72.

8. Gallarus: A Nest Beside Thy Altar

148–49 *Writing about Celtic spirituality* ... : Noel Dermot O'Donoghue, *The Mountain Behind the Mountain: Aspects of the Celtic Tradition* (Edinburgh: T&T Clark, 1993).

149 *"When I am liberated by silence . . .":* Thomas Merton, *Thoughts in Solitude* (New York: Farrar, Straus and Cudahy, 1958), pp. 93–94.

150 *"a prayer of silence, simplicity . . .":* Thomas Merton, *Contemplative Prayer* (New York: Herder and Herder, 1969), p. 33.

151 *"Life showers over everything, radiant, gushing":* Diane Ackerman, *A Natural History of the Senses* (New York: Random House, 1990), p. xvii.

157 *But every double-blind experiment . . . :* I examined the medical study of Dr. Randolph Byrd, and the books of Larry Dossey and other New Age gurus; there is less there than meets the eye.

158 *"We should not think . . .":* Eriugena quoted by Carey, *A Single Ray of the Sun,* p. 80.

161 *"My first thought was . . .":* Charles Francis Hall quoted by Candace Savage, *Aurora* (San Francisco: Sierra Club Books, 1994), p. 78.

162 *"Let us go on and on endlessly . . .":* Pierre Teilhard de Chardin, *Hymn of the Universe* (New York: Harper and Row, 1961), p. 79.

164 *Father John Casey . . . :* The story is drawn from MacDonogh, *The Dingle Peninsula,* pp. 129–30. MacDonogh's source is Breandán Breathnach, *Dancing in Ireland* (Dal gCais, 1983).

166 *"In the 'prayer of the heart' . . .":* Merton, *Contemplative Prayer,* p. 82.

167 *"[The] mind is illumined . . .":* John Cassian quoted by Merton, *Contemplative Prayer,* p. 57.

167 *"the light at the center of every cell":* Mary Oliver, *New and Selected Poems* (Boston: Beacon Press, 1992), p. 184.

INDEX

A

Absolute 159
  quest for encounter with
    162
Ackerman, Diane 151
Adam and Eve 96–97, 103, 142
Adam's sin 113, 115
Africa 8–9, 107
Age of Enlightenment 110
Age of Saints and Scholars xi,
  134
Airplane Valley 66, 112
Alexandria/Alexandrians 90,
  100, 133
  empiricism 98
  science 97
All Saints' Day 25, 31
All Souls' Day 31
Alps 9, 13, 18, 85
Altus Prosator (Exalted Creator)
  111
Ambiguity 39–40
Amergin 76, 81, 113, 123, 124,
  144, 148, 168
America 55
  discovery of, by Brendan 6,
    130–31
Ammonite fossils 92
Anascaul 88
Anascaul Lake 88
Animals 52, 89

Animism 79, 100
Antinous 45
Apple tree 3
Aran Islands 102
Archimedes 72, 90
Ardfert diocese 22
Aristarchus 90–91
Aristotle 72, 90, 91, 107
Arthur, King 3
Artifacts 47, 70, 154, 155
  Dingle Peninsula 156
  Mount Brandon 19, 111–12
Ascoli, Prince D' 129
Astronomically aligned tombs
  90
Astronomy 91, 114, 133
  mathematical 29–30
Athena 79
Atlantic fringe 69, 71, 72, 73,
  141
  worldview of people on
    103–4
Atlantic Ocean
  birth of 120
  first solo air crossing 128
  sailing into 57
  visitors from 129
  widening 120–21
Augustine 96
Augustine of Hippo, Saint 89,
  137

Aurora borealis   160–62

Avalon (Island of Apples)   3

Azores   6, 152

Azores Anticyclone   54

B

Ball, John   85

Ballybrack   ix, 9, 34, 110

Ballydavid   160

Ballydavid Head   119

Ballymore Sandstone Formation   107

Beaker people   70

Bealtaine   31, 32–33

Beatitudes   11

Bed of Diarmaid and Grainne   77

Belenus   32–33

Bencorr   102

Berry, Thomas   139–40, 141

Bible   95, 141

Big Bang   142

Binn na Port (Peak of the Fort)   65–69, 71–72, 73, 75, 76, 81–82, 84, 85

Biology   114

Birds   56

   from the west   54–55

Blasket Islands   19, 51

Blasket Sound   128–29

Blathnaid   68

Blessed Western Isles   55–56

Board of Works   17

Boats   20, 126, 131–32

Book of Invasions   74

Book of Kells   76

Boulders   18, 85, 88

Boyne culture   70

Bran   4, 5, 10, 59

   stories of   58

   voyage to Land of the Women   2–3, 26, 131

Brandon (village)   4

Brandon Bay   9, 22, 30, 44, 65, 76, 112

Brandon Creek   20, 130

Brandon Head   20, 131

Brandon Point   3, 4

Brendan   130

Brendan, Saint (the Navigator)   5–6, 10, 11, 15, 18, 45, 50, 61, 107, 110, 111, 115, 151

   attempt to repeat sea voyage of   130–31

   background   48–49

   and Crom Dubh   23, 34–35, 38, 47

   death of   153

   diocese   22

   feast day   9

   hermitage   19, 34, 96

   and mountains   12–13

   solitude on Mount Brandon before voyage   19, 112, 113, 152

   statue of   45, 59, 62

   voyage in search of Isles of the Blest   6, 8, 20, 58, 133, 136, 138

Brendan Voyage, The (Severin)   131

Brigit   32, 61–62

Brittany   118

Broecker, Wallace   54

Bronze Age   11, 29, 31, 69, 70

Byron, George Gordon   13, 20

C

Caherconree   68
Calcification   78, 79, 80, 81
Calpornius   46
Canada   54
Candlemas Day   25
Canonical hours   36
Cape Verde Islands   6
Carey, John   93, 95, 96, 97–98, 99, 103, 111, 124, 134, 137, 145
Caribbean Sea   53
Carrantuohill   5, 9, 64
Cartography/cartographers   16, 101
Casey, John   164
Cassian, John   167
Cathedrals   30, 31
Catholicism   7, 37
Cattle   31–32
Ceall Ide   49
Celtic Christianity   40, 45, 88
  ideas of, sent to Europe 132–33
Celtic migration   32–33, 35
Celtic myths   7, 35
  violence in   73
Celtic revival   60
Celtic spirituality   73, 82, 148–49
Celtic stories
  in written language   57
Celtic traditions   39–40
Celts
  gods of   40, 41, 58
  invasions   69
  pagan associations   32

stories of   59
  see also Pre-Christian Celts
Certainty, arrogance of   122
Cessair   70
Charles the Bald   158
Christendom, wild fringe of 135
Christian era   45, 69 90, 122
Christianity   35–41, 61
  continental   60, 88, 155
  creation in   92
  Crom Dubh converted to 34–35
  defining question for 95–96
  encounter with paganism 57–58
  enemy of landscape   155
  in Europe   134
  in Ireland   74–75
  Ireland's conversion to   xi, 48, 59, 124
  and nature   90, 149
  overwhelmed Celtic paganism   50–51
  and pantheism   156, 159
  paradise of   71
  Romans and   79
  and science   91
  see also Irish Christianity
Christians
  see Early Irish Christians; Irish Christians; Mediterranean Christianity
Christmas   24
Church
  centralized   98
  continental   158–59
  institutional   133

Circadian rhythms   27–28

Climate   24, 52–54

Climbers   x, 10, 14, 15–16, 17–18, 19–20

Cloghane   4, 44

   church at   29, 30, 33, 40–41, 46

   "pattern" at   34

   stone head   22–23, 40–41, 46

Clonfert   49

Cloonsharragh   29–30

Cluain na Fola (Field of Blood) 127

Colum Cille   39, 61, 111

Columbanus, Saint   82, 100, 103, 115, 122, 123, 151

   creation in   94–95

Columbus, Christopher   131

Connacht   4–5

Connemara   11, 102

Connor Pass   18

Consciousness   142

Constantine   37, 38, 79, 94, 98, 135

Continent (the)

   intellectual link to   90

   transcendent theology of 93

Continents   144

   moving   87, 106, 119–20, 121

Cornwall   118

Cosmic time   113–14

Cosmology   140

Coumaknock (mountain hollow)   69, 84, 85, 86, 97, 103, 107

   climb out of   109–10

   strata of   92

Council of Nicaea   58

County Derry   101

County Galway   49

County Kerry   4, 22

Creation   87, 89, 94

   canonical stories of   137

   celebrating   124

   in Christianity   92

   Creator in/and   96, 98, 158

   in geologic time   108–9

   God in   141

   responsibility for   159

   scientific story of   139–40, 141–44, 149

   voice of   167

   years allotted to   115

Creation stories   87–88, 103

Creator   87

   action of   95–96

   in/and creation   98, 158

   nature primary revelation of 115, 122–23

Croagh Patrick   5, 10, 11, 72

Crom Dubh (Black Crom)   23, 24, 33, 34, 38, 47, 76

   converted to Christianity 34–35

   magical powers   40

   stone head   41, 46

Cromwell, Oliver   4

Cross slabs   50

Cross stones   112, 154

Cross-days   31–33

Cross-inscribed stones   14–15, 16, 112

Cross-quarter days   25

Crossbedding   87, 106

Cu Chulainn   68, 88, 142

Cu Roi   68, 85

Cuill, Mac   126
Cúin na dtréan Fhir (Slaughter of Mighty Men)   127
Cultural sea change   16–17
Curiosity   93, 104, 138
Curraghs   20, 130

D

Dancing at Lughnasa (Friel)   31
Dante   97, 101
Death   70–71, 73
    sea physical analogue for 136
Demonization   134
Diarmaid   72–73, 74
Dingle Bay   9, 14, 102, 128
Dingle Peninsula   ix, 4, 5, 8, 19, 68, 153
    artifacts   156
    circular stone habitations 154
    end of   110, 119, 135–36, 150
    Gallarus   152
    mapping of   64, 108
    ridges   119
    ring forts   154–55
    rocks of   106
    souterrains   118
    survey of antiquities of   65
    visitors from the sea 127–28
    watchtowers   129
    weather on   51
Dingle town   ix, x
    girls school in   49
Dingle Way   15
Dionysus   79

"Discovery of a New Devonian Tetrapod Trackway in SW Ireland, The"   108
Divine Comedy (Dante)   101
DNA   123, 124, 149
Domhnach Crom Dubh (Crom Dubh Sunday)   34
Drake, Francis   129
Druids   79, 124, 148
    deities of   134
    and human sacrifice   73
    nature worship merged with Mediterranean Christianity   152
    pantheism   155
    tradition of   137, 139
Drumlins   85
Du Noyer, George Victor   64, 108
Dublin   73
Dún an Óir (Fort of Gold) 128
Dun Cinn Tire   66–67
Dunmore Head   119

E

Eamhain Abhlach (Land of Apples)   3
Early Irish Christians   20, 141, 145
    God of   148–49
    and miracles   136–38
    see also Irish Christianity
Earth   23–24, 26, 91, 103, 123, 144
    creation of   92
    crust   9, 106, 119
    history of   107–8

Earth (*continued*)
    magnetic field 161
    Sun and 77
Earth mother 61
East Africa 109
Easter 24
Ecological consciousness 103, 155, 156
Eighty-Fourth Psalm 159
Elizabeth I 128
Empirical knowledge
    and traditional faith x
Empiricism x, 81, 144
    Alexandrian 98
England 85
English Channel 135
Enlightenment 13, 16, 17, 18, 20, 102, 113, 155
    Irish Church resisted 156
Equinoxes 24–25, 31
    stone structures aligned to 25–26
Érainn 68
Eratosthenes 90, 101
Erc, Bishop 48–49
Eriksson, Leif 131
Eriugena 158–59
Erosion 9, 108, 114
Eskers 85
Eucharist 98
Euclid 72
Eudoxus 91
Euhemerism 134
Eurasia 69
Europe 8, 9, 93
    Celtic Christianity in 132–33, 134
    collision with Africa 107
    North America moving away from 120, 121

Eve, sin of 60
    see also Adam and Eve

F

Faeroes 136, 152
Faha (village) 9, 17, 34, 44, 107, 112
    ascent from 64
    pilgrim path 11, 84, 110
    shrine at 59, 62
Fairy faith (*creideamh sí*) 132, 134
Fairy folk 99–100, 118–19, 135, 139, 148
Fairy forts 17, 155
Faith 140
    and empirical knowledge x
    science and 139
    shift from vertical to horizontal 7–8
    yielded to reason 13–14
Fall equinox 25
Febal (king) 2
Fenian Cycle 74
Fenit 58
Ferris, Timothy 115, 117
Festivals 31–34, 90
Fianna 56–57, 69, 74, 127
Firbolgs 70
Fire in the head 76, 77–78, 81, 144, 149
Food Vessel people 70
Forts
    fairy 17, 155
    hill-top 49–50
    see also Promontory forts; Ring forts
Fossils 91, 92, 106, 108

Fosterage 49

Fothar na Manaigh (the green fields of the monk) 48

Friel, Brian 31

G

Gaelic folkore and language 5

Gaels 70

Galen 80

Galileo 90, 99, 100

Gallarus 152, 153–54

Gallarus Oratory 153–54, 156, 159–62, 162–63, 168

Genesis 87, 88, 92, 96
  literal interpretation of 107, 115

Geographic role (Mount Brandon) 99–100

Geography 133
  horizontal 17
  physical and spiritual 19, 20
  supernatural 16

Geologic history of Ireland x

Geologic time 107–8, 113–15
  discovery of 108–9, 115, 116

Geological Guide to the Dingle Peninsula (Horne) 64

Geological Survey of Ireland 64
  Dingle Bay sheet 106, 108

Geology 18, 91–93, 102–3, 106–7, 108, 113, 114, 115, 120
  beginning of 13

Gerald of Wales 52–53, 61, 88–89

Giant's Bed 26

Glacial corries 82, 84, 86–87

Glaciers 9, 18, 19, 70, 84, 85, 102, 144, 150

Glenbeigh 56

Gnostic spiritualism 98

God
  of Christianity 36, 38–39, 45, 100
  concepts of 7–8
  in creation 141
  of early Irish Christians 148–49
  interventions by 89, 137, 162
  manifest in everyday life 132
  in nature 98, 137, 151
  as person 165
  personal 140, 148
  praying to 157, 158
  problem of evil 158, 159
  relationship with world 94
  separate from creation 37

Gods 71
  ancient 10, 134
  anthropomorphic 109
  of Celts 40, 41, 58
  Greco-Roman 139
  in nature 76–77
  pagan 134–35, 139
  of pre-Christian Celts 35
  of Romans 37, 79

Golden Rule 74

Goodenough, Ursula 143

Grace, perception as 151

Grainne 72–73, 74

Grand Banks of Newfoundland 53–54

Great Blasket Islands 119, 136

Greeks
    geologic time   113
    gods   79, 139
Greenland   139
Grey, Lord, of Wilton   128
Griffith, Richard   108
Groundhog Day   25, 31
Gulf of Mexico   53
Gulf Stream   53–54

Horne, Ralph   64
Human history   109, 113
Human mind   78, 139, 141
Human sacrifice   31, 73
Humanity
    common   81
    essence of   143
Humans   77–78
Hutton, James   107, 108, 113–14

H

Hadrian, Emperor   45
Hall, Charles Francis   161
Hall, James   114
Halloween   25, 31, 32
Hamsters   28
Hanukkah   24
Hawking, Stephen   116
Hawthorne   3–4
Headwall   18, 19, 86, 97, 110
Heaney, Seamus   160
Heaven   7, 8, 16, 36, 55–56, 101, 138, 151
    sailing westward to find   57
Hebrides   136
Hell   101
Hibernicus, Augustinus ("Irish Augustine")   99, 103, 121–22, 123, 124, 137–38
Hilda, Saint   92–93
Hildoceras   92
Hill of Tara   4
Hindus   79
Holy men and women   10, 72, 144
Holy mountains   10–11, 72
Holy wells   112, 163, 164
    of Brendan   34, 144

I

Iapetus (ocean)   106
Ice   82, 85
    see also Glaciers
Ice ages   18, 85
Iceland   54, 136, 139
Ignorance   121, 137, 144
    discovery of   115–17
Imbolc   31, 32, 61
Immanence   6, 13, 93, 132, 136, 138, 144
    prayer and   149
    and problem of evil   158
    and transcendence   7–8, 94, 134, 149
Incarnation   36, 98
Indian Ocean   54
Inishnabro   119, 136
Inishtooskert   119
Inishvickillane   119
Inquisition   138
Insight   167
Intellectual commerce   132
Intellectual revolution   16–17
Ireland   85, 99
    Christian presence in   38
    conversion to Christianity   xi, 48, 59, 124

ideas coming to   132

invasions in history of   47,
    69–70

mapping of   16, 101–2

souterrains   118

Irish (the)   x

intellectually advanced   72

scholarly people   48

see also Pre-Christian
    Ireland/Irish

Irish Christian writings

nature in   113

Irish Christianity   93–95, 98

unique character of   39

Irish Christians   74–75, 82

God of   89

see also Early Irish
    Christians

Irish Church

resistance to Enlightenment
    thought   156

Irish culture, transformation of
    50–51

Irish landscape, map of
    100–1

Irish myths   7, 87–88

death in   71

invasions in   69–70

rediscovered   60–61

sources of   58

see also Celtic myths

Irish Sea   132, 135

Iron Age   11, 69, 70

Islam   71

Isle of Man   68

Isles of the Blest   6–7, 45

Ita   49, 59

Iveragh Peninsula   106

J

Jason and the Argonauts   130

Jellyfish   129

Jesus Christ   11, 34, 58, 74, 159

divinity   98

rising from dead   37

Jukes, Joseph Beete   108

Jupiter   30, 79

K

Kerry   51, 53, 89

plants   52

winds   54

Kerry County Council   44

Kerry Mountaineering Club
    44

Kerry mountains   11, 12

Kilcolman (church of Colman)
    14–15, 16–17

Kildare, nuns of   61

Killarney   56

Killorglin, County Kerry   33

Kilmalkedar   47

King Cycle   74

King of France   127, 128

Knockanaffrin (Mountain of the
    Mass)   12

L

Labrador Current   54

Lake District   13

Lammas   25

Land of Delight   6–7, 19, 55,
    71, 77, 113, 138

Land of Saints and Scholars   99

Land of the Women   2, 5, 26

Laoghaire, King   148

Lapa na circe (hen's foot)   16

Large-flowered butterworts   86

Late-Neolithic culture   70

Latin language   46, 47, 49

Legends   74–75

Leiden   33

Life after death   70–71

Light of the World   34, 36, 38

Lindbergh, Charles   128, 129

Lough Foyle   101

Lucifer   134

Lucretius   72

Lug   35, 38, 45, 76
  Christianized ritual   33–34

Lughnasa ("feast of Lug")   31, 33, 76

Lusitanian flora and fauna   52, 127

Lyon   33

M

Mac Cumhail, Fionn   56, 73, 85, 127, 133–34, 142

MacDonogh, Steve   67, 69, 71

Macgillicuddy Reeks   5, 64

MacNeill, Máire   33, 34–35

Maharee Islands   65

Mám na Gaoithe (Windy Gap)   128

Manchan, Saint   163

Map of Ireland   101–2

Mapmaking, mathematical   100–1

Mars   79

Martyrdom   37, 55, 56, 57, 124

Mary, cult of   61

"Mass stone"   12

Mathematical astronomy   29–30

Matter   37, 96

Matthew   11

May Day   25, 31, 33, 39

Mayo   10

Mediterranean   51
  learning of   152

Mediterranean, eastern   39
  monotheism of   57–58
  science of   90

Mediterranean Christianity   36, 45, 55–56, 98
  merged with druidic nature worship   152

Megalithic movements   29

Merton, Thomas   149, 151, 156, 166, 167

Metaphoric thinking   78, 80, 81

Metaphorical role (Mount Brandon)   99–100

Middle Ages   49

Middle East   98, 137

Milesians   70, 75

Milky Way Galaxy   23

Milton, John   96–97

Mimosa plant   27

Miracles   37, 88, 89, 92, 95, 98, 133, 136–38, 162
  in continental Church   158
  examination of   157
  in nature's laws   99

Misogyny   59, 60

Mistletoe   39

Monarch butterflies   55

Monasteries   13, 48, 49, 50
  on coastal islands   152
  founded in Europe by Irish   93

Monks   6, 7, 19, 87, 95, 144
  of Gallarus   162
  introduced written language
    to Ireland   35
  and mountains   13
  sea voyages   131–32, 139
  settled on islands   136
  and sexual desire   59
  on Skellig Michael   150–51,
    152
Monotheism   x, 39, 93, 100
  Judeo-Christian   51
  and polytheism   57–58
Moon   23, 30, 51, 87, 91, 123
  knowledge of   90
Moraines   18, 85
Moses   10
Mount Brandon   xi, 3, 5–6, 7,
    11, 17–20, 30, 48, 62, 72
  ascent of/climbing   ix–x,
    34, 44–45, 64–65, 84, 86,
    107
  holy mountain   10
  latitude   26
  paths   9, 17–18, 64–65
  plants   52
  roles of   99–100
  skeletal structure of   86
  summit   ix, 10, 14, 17, 20,
    86, 102, 110, 111–13, 119,
    120, 129–30, 144
  summit: Brendan on   48,
    152
  summit: flora   123
  summit: pilgrimage to   15
  valleys   18, 85
  wearing down   120
Mount Eagle   19, 119
Mount of Purgatorio   97
Mount Sinai   10
Mount Zion   10–11

Mountain gloom/mountain
  glory   13, 14, 20, 60, 96, 102,
    110
Mountaineering/mountaineers
  13, 97
Mountains   4–5, 11–14, 109,
    144, 149
  celebration of   13
  explanation of   108
  fearful places   11, 96, 97
  highest   5
  holy   10–11, 72
  natural origin of   20
  as places of refuge   11–12
  shunned by Europeans   12,
    13
  wearing down   120
Munster   5
Music of What Happens, The
  (Ó Ríordáin)   133–34
Muslims   79
Mystery   xi, 97, 123, 136, 156,
    162
  knowledge and   124
  need for   139
  prayer and   149
  responses to   78, 81
Mystery (the)   124
Mystery of Mysteries   103
Mystery without science/science
  without mystery   138
Myths   29, 74
  see also Celtic myths; Irish
    myths

N

NaoíGhiallach, Niall (Niall of
  the Nine Hostages)   47
Native Americans   79

Natural history of Ireland   x,
  52, 88–89
Natural History of the Senses, A
  (Ackerman)   151
Natural law   89, 90, 138, 158
Natural philosophers   18, 90, 91
Naturalistic view of world   99
Nature   73, 98–99
  Christianity and   149
  communion with   72
  consciousness of   103–4
  corrupted   96
  divine in   89, 95
  enchanted   135
  fallen state of   132, 155
  geologic time and   115
  God in   98, 151, 173
  gods in   76–77
  God's works and   121–22
  history of   115
  integrity of   124
  interest in   90
  in Irish Christian writings
    113
  laws of   116
  observation of   90–91
  patterns of   37
  phenomena of   123
  rediscovered by reason   97
  is sacred   156
  traditions of   137–38
*Navigatio Sancti Brendani,
  Abbatis* (Voyage of Saint
  Brendan, Abbot)   45, 130,
  131, 133
Near East   36
Neart   151, 155, 162
Nemed   70
New England   85
New Story   139–40, 141–44, 149
New Testament   11

Newfoundland   110, 131
Newgrange   25, 29
Newton, Isaac   85, 90, 99
Niamh   56, 58, 59, 60, 74, 142,
  143
Nicaea   98
  doctrines of   94
Nicholson, Marjorie Hope   12,
  13, 96, 97, 113
Noah   12, 92
Norman incursions   60
North America   8, 53, 119
  move away from Europe
    120, 121
  Severin's voyage to   131
North Atlantic   53, 136
North Atlantic Drift   54

O

Ó Duinn, Seán   132, 134
Ó hÓgáin, Dáithi   78, 100
Ó Ríordáin, John   133–34
O'Donoghue, Noel Dermot
  148–49
Ogham script   15, 46, 74, 118
Oisin   56–57, 58, 59, 60, 74, 142,
  143
Old Red Sandstone cliffs   129
Old Red Sandstone Continent
  8, 87, 106, 107, 119
  strata of   114
Old Testament   11, 96, 114
Oliver, Mary   167
On the Miracles of Holy Scripture
  (Hibernicus)   99, 121–22,
  137–38
Oratio ignita (fiery prayer)   167
Oratory(ies)   6, 10, 163
  see also Gallarus Oratory

Ordnance Survey of Ireland
16, 19, 66, 102, 112

Origen   89–90

Original Sin   12, 45, 135, 137

Orkneys   136

Otherworld   56

   Celtic   40

   spiritual   133

Ovid   72

Owenmore River   18, 65, 84,
85

Owennafeana River (river of the
Fianna)   66

Oxford English Dictionary   79

P

Pacific Ocean   54

Paganism   36, 93

   encounter with Christianity
39, 50–51, 57–58

Pagels, Heinz   117

Panama, isthmus at   53

Pantheism   77, 94, 98, 111, 113,
132, 138, 158

   in/and Christianity   156,
159

   remnants of   155

Papal Taxation List   22

Paradise   6, 7, 71, 134

   Brendan's search for   20

Paradise Lost (Milton)   96–97

Parthalon   70

Particle accelerating machines
142

Patrick   11, 50, 58, 60, 61,
74–75, 90, 92, 126, 151

   banishing Crom Dubh   34

   converted Ireland to
Christianity   xi

   God of   148

   mountain of   10

   and mountains   12–13

   reached Ireland   38

   return to Ireland   22, 47,
48, 57

   statue of   45, 59, 62

   writings of   89

   written language   46–47

"Pattern"   33–34, 163–64

Pax Romana   36

Peddler's Lake   18

Perception   151

Philip of Spain, King   129

Phoenician sailors   6

Physical geography   x, 19

Physics   114

Pilgrim path   84, 85–86

Pilgrims/pilgrimages   9, 10, 14,
15–16, 34, 44, 72

Pillars of Hercules (Straits of
Gibraltor)   6

Planetary motion   91

Planets   23, 51

Plants   52

Plato   72

Playfair, John   114, 116

Pliny the Elder   91, 96

Plutarch   79

Polytheism   x, 39, 77, 79, 93

   and monotheism   57–58

Popper, Karl   116

Portraiture in stone   45–46

Praeger, Robert Lloyd   85

Prayer   149–50, 156–57, 168

   attentive   166–67

   efficacy of   157, 158

   expression of wonder,
thanksgiving, praise
157–58

   places built for   152–54

Pre-Celtic peoples, story cycles of   141
Pre-Christian Celts   99–100
    gods of   35
    knowledge of nature   90–91
    places of worship   30–31
    world view   109
Pre-Christian Ireland/Irish
    religious beliefs   78, 79
    story cycles   141
    tales of   60–61
Presence, perception of   148
Priests   90, 124
Problem of evil   158–59
Promontory forts   11–12, 66, 68, 128
Protestant Reformation   98
Protestantism   7–8, 37
Psalter of the Quatrains, The   95–96
Ptolemy, Claudius   101
Puck Fair   33–34
Punishment of lawbreakers   126–27
Punxsutawney, Pennsylvania   25
Purgatory   101

R

Radiation detectors   142
Raleigh, Walter   128
Rationalism   155
Reask   50, 154
Reason   xi, 13, 139
    faith yielded to   14
    nature redeemed by   97
    and superstition   78
Red admiral butterflies   67

Red Branch Cycle   74
Redemption   159
Reek Sunday   10
Religion   78, 81, 134, 140, 143
    of celebration and praise   132
    pre-Christian Celts   30–31, 100
    at Reask   154
    and science   138
    and solar cycles   36
    Sun-centered   26–27
    of theology   132–33
    Western Sea as source of Celtic   135–36
Religious festivals   31–34
Religious practices   29, 93–94
Renaissance   91
Resurrection of the body   36, 138
Righ na nDúl   149
Ring forts   50, 117–18, 154–55
Rock of Cashel   4
Roman Catholic theology   151
Roman Church   38, 94, 98, 137, 138
Roman Empire   37–38, 98
Roman gods   37, 79
Romanticism   20
Rome/Romans   37–38, 45–46, 138
    superstition   79, 80

S

Sacred Depths of Nature, The (Goodenough)   143
Saint Brendan's Oratory   112
Saint Brigit's Day   61

St. John's Eve   24

Saint Patrick's cabbage   52

St. Patrick's Day   25

Saints   x, 10, 111, 148

Saint's Road   15

Salome   60

Samain   31–32

Santa Maria de la Rosa (galleon)   129

Satan   92

Satellite Laser Ranging   120

Saturn   30

Sauce Creek   114

Scal ni Mhurnain   88

Science   41, 81, 90–91, 95, 118–19, 139, 142

    Christianity and   133

    and Irish Christianity   93

    modern   117

    "new"   99

    religion and   138

    and spiritual values   140

    and superstition   80–81

Scientific ecology   155

Scientific method   81, 90–91

Scientific Revolution   16, 97, 98–99

Scotland   118

Scripture   94, 121

    miracles of   99, 137

    mountain imagery of   11

    replaced   13

Sea (the)   51, 56, 123, 126, 135

    incursions from   128–29

Self   164–65

Sermon on the Mount   159

Severin, Tim   130–31, 133, 136, 139

Sex   59, 77

Shanakeel (Old Church)   6, 48

Shetlands   136, 152

Sinbad the Sailor   130

Skellig Michael   19, 72, 150–51, 152, 153

    oratory   152

Skinner, B. F.   80

Slieve Mish Mountains   68

Smerwick Harbor   64, 119, 128, 160

Smyth, Marina   90, 104, 137

Solar cycles   29, 36

Solar observations   29–30

Solar system   23–24

Solstices   31

    stone structures aligned to   25–26

"Song of Amergin" ("The Mystery")   75–76, 81, 165–66

Souterrains   118

South America   53

South Equatorial Current   53

Spanish Armada   128–29

Spectroscopes   142

Spirit of St. Louis   128

Spiritual geography   x, 19

Spirituality

    Celtic   73, 82, 148–49

    scientific   140–41

Spring equinox   24–25

Standing stones   90, 155

    Cloonsharragh   29–30

    cross-inscribed   47

Starry Night Pro   29–30

Stars   87, 90

Steno, Nicolaus   107

Stone Age   70

Stone circles   26, 30, 31, 90

Stone structures

    aligned to solstices, and equinoxes   25–26, 30, 31

Stonehenge   25, 29, 31
Stories   141, 142, 144
    canonical   137
    true   142–43
Storytelling   35, 39, 77
    women in   59
Stradbally Mountain   65
Summer solstice   29
Sun   23, 24, 32, 38, 51, 76, 87,
    91, 123, 161
    claim on human history
        28–29
    cycles of   35
    and Earth   77
    and festivals   24–27
    knowledge of   90
    return of   32
    in setting   56
    standing stones aligned to
        29–30, 31
Supernatural   37
    shift to natural   16
Superstition   37, 78–81
    fairytales as   155
Suprachiasmatic nuclei (SCN)
    28
Switzerland   85
Sybil Head   119
Synod of Whitby   92

Telescopes   142
Tennyson, Alfred Lord   110–11
This or that dilemmas   39–40
Three Sisters   119
Tir na nOg   56–57, 58, 77
toothache   40–41
Topography of Ireland   4
Tralee   5, 48
Tralee Bay   58
Transcendence   45, 88, 93, 95,
    132, 133, 136
    in continental Church   158
    and immanence   7–8, 94,
        134, 149
Transubstantiation   36, 98
Tuatha De Danann   70
Twelve Bens of Connemara   5

U

Ulysses   130
Universe   103
    age of   109, 116
    response to   144
    scientific knowledge of   119
    is unity   140
Uplift   108, 114
Upper Paleozoic era   106
Urn people   70
Ussher, James   92, 107

T

Tara   49
Taur Mountain   102
Tearaght (island)   110, 119, 136
Tearaght Rock   51
Technological civilization   142
Teilhard de Chardin, Pierre
    162, 167

V

Valentia Island   128
Ventry Beach   129
Ventry Harbor   127
Venus   30

Vertical to horizontal shift
7–8, 16
Very Long Baseline
Interferometry   120–21
Vikings   136, 153
  invasions   60, 88
Vinci, Leonardo da   107
Violence   73–74
Virgin, shrine of   9, 17, 45, 62
Voltaire   78

W

Warriors   x, 10, 18
Weather   51–54, 69
Western civilization, defining
question for   95–96
Western culture   x, 37
Western Sea   6, 19, 77, 100
  Brendan's voyage in   58
  excursions on   152

idea of Land of Delight in
71
source of Celtic religious
thought   135–36
stories of voyages on   131
Western voyages of discovery
7, 26, 136, 138
Where Three Streams Meet
(Ó Duinn)   132
Whitby, England   92
Wilson, Edward O.   139
Winter solstice   24
Women   59–60
Wonder, sense of   162
Wordsworth, William   13, 20,
156
World War II   66, 112
Worldviews   103–4
  Celtic   109
  conflict between   138
Written language   46, 47–48
  Celtic stories in   57
  power of   35